IN SEARCH OF REVENGE AND RESPECT

TIMOTHY M. FARABAUGH

IN SEARCH OF REVENGE AND RESPECT

SECOND EDITION

TATE PUBLISHING
AND ENTERPRISES, LLC

Published by Tate Publishing & Enterprises, LLC
127 E. Trade Center Terrace | Mustang, Oklahoma 73064 USA
1.888.361.9473 | www.tatepublishing.com

Tate Publishing is committed to excellence in the publishing industry. The company reflects the philosophy established by the founders, based on Psalm 68:11,
"The Lord gave the word and great was the company of those who published it."

Book design copyright © 2014 by Tate Publishing, LLC. All rights reserved.
Interior design by Jimmy Sevilleno

Published in the United States of America

ISBN: 978-1-62746-797-1
1. History / United States / Colonial Period (1600-1775)
14.01.03

This book is dedicated to my wife who continues to be a source of encouragement. I would like to thank her, my daughter and granddaughter who endured visits to forts, battlefields and museums as I gathered research material for this book.

CHAPTER ONE

These were troubling times for the people living around Fort Bedford. Indians had been raiding homes, farms and entire communities. It wasn't just the Bedford area that was experiencing problems with the Indians either. From Berks and Northampton counties in Pennsylvania all the way down to the Shenandoah Valley in Virginia there were scenes of death and destruction. People were terrified of Indian attacks because of the gruesome stories that had been repeated. They seemed almost unbelievable. People everywhere were talking about someone's house or barn being burned and those who were killed or taken off into the woods never to be seen again. What was happening was unusual and frightening. The settlers who had moved west from Philadelphia and other east coast cities expected hardship, but not the kind of terror they currently lived with every day.

Gus was a young man who had moved to Fort Bedford with his parents, and he was amazed at the stories he had heard. He and his friend George, who lived nearby, were out hunting in the woods between their homes when George asked, "Did you hear about the Leininger family who lived near Penns Creek?"

"No, where is that?" replied Gus.

"Oh, its north east of here along the Susquehanna River." continued George. "My Pa told me that the whole settlement at Penns Creek was wiped out by Indians. The father of the family was shot and the oldest boy was tomahawked right across the head. He said that fourteen people were killed and eleven more are missing. One was a ten year old girl named Regina that everyone thinks was taken by the Indians."

"What about the Ma, was she one of the ones who was killed?" asked Gus.

"No." replied George. "The Ma and youngest boy escaped the raid and their certain death by being in the grist mill at the time. She searched and searched after the attack, but found no sign of Regina. She didn't know if it were better to pray that she remain alive in the hands of the Indians, or dead. People say she has nearly gone out of her mind."

Gus sat in silence after hearing that. He was disturbed by all the tales of death and destruction that he had recently heard. This new story made him angry at the Indians who had never posed a threat before that he knew of, but recently, they were coming around killing innocent men, women and children. He knew there had been a war going on between the British and the French along with some of the Indian tribes who were friendly with them several years ago, but that didn't mean the Indians should come over the mountains and kill. It just didn't seem right somehow. It made no sense to him.

After thinking about all of this for a few minutes he asked, "Did your Pa say why the Indians have been raiding these settlements?"

"No. He just said that we all needed to be prepared. Even though we live near the fort; that might not stop these blood-thirsty Indians." replied George.

"Do you think they would come around here?" Gus asked.

"I don't know, but my Pa told me to carry my musket with me when I was going away from home. You better do the same. You just never know what will happen, and a fella with a musket just might be able to scare off a few Indians."

"Well, I have a fine one and I'll be happy to show them how it works if it comes down to it. I just do not understand why they would begin to act this way." said Gus.

"Me either, but just be prepared." replied George.

"I will. You do the same. I'll tell my parents about the Leininger family." said Gus.

The conversation was interrupted by a noise ahead of them in the woods. Something or someone was coming their way. Both boys brought their muskets to their shoulders. In a few seconds, a mother deer and her baby appeared. The young men looked at each other and decided not to shoot.

Gus said, "Go on for now, little deer. When I see you next year, you'll be a big buck. Then I'll have you for dinner!"

The boys laughed and started on their way home. It was getting dark and their mothers would be expecting them soon. They would come back again another day to see if they could find a deer for dinner.

When Gus got home from his unsuccessful day of hunting with George he told his parents about the story George had shared. They had already heard the story from some of the neighbors, but his father assured him that since Penns Creek was so far away, and they lived near a fort, the Indians would not come to their area. Their reassurances made Gus feel a little better but he decided to take his musket with him if he left the farm just in case.

CHAPTER TWO

Gus had gone to school through the 6th grade so he could learn to read and write English and do arithmetic. His parents still spoke German better than English, but Gus was able to speak both languages well enough to get by.

His father told him, "It is important to be able to speak the language of the people you live with and even if you are going to be a farmer, you must learn your sums." And so he went to school just long enough to get the basics. He was not very good in school, though he passed all his classes each year. He would sooner be out hunting or fishing than spelling, reading or solving math problems.

Gus' parents were German immigrants. Like others in this area, his father had cleared some land several years ago and planted his first field of corn. Each year they cleared more land and planted more corn and hay. The broader fields that Gus and his father now worked yielded an abundance of hay for the animals and corn for roasting, bread and cakes. His mother had a vegetable garden next to the house. She grew peas, beans, squash, onions and a few root vegetables like turnips, carrots and potatoes. And like many of the Germans around them, they grew cabbages that they were able to make into a favorite dish called sauerkraut. Gus loved his mother's sauerkraut, especially when she cooked it with pork ribs from the pigs they raised. Along with the pigs, Gus' family raised chickens and had a few cows for milking.

Their lives were not easy. Everyone worked. As a result, they were able to grow, make, hunt for or buy all the essentials like meats, sugar, salt, and a supply of coarse cloths to wear. For the most part, they were self-sufficient.

Gus and his family were not fancy in any way. He and his father wore shirts that were made of heavy linen, overalls most of the time, but breeches on special occasions, a vest, woolen socks, which had been hand-knit by his mother, and a pair of common shoes made to fit either foot. To top their outfits off, Gus and his father wore the popular three cornered hats some folks called a "cocked-hat" that was made of black felt. Gus's mother wore a plain long dress with an apron. When she went outside, she often wore a bonnet on her head. This is what most people wore. Gus didn't feel any different than any of the other young people who lived around him. No one seemed to have much. Everyone worked hard to make a living. And neighbors helped neighbors when times were difficult.

Fortunately, the area around Fort Bedford was rich in wildlife. There was a wide variety, including black bear, wolves, and panthers that some folks called mountain lions, white tailed deer, quail, ruffled grouse, pheasant, rabbit, squirrel and flocks of turkey. When he was younger, he wasn't allowed to go too far away without his father being with him, but when they were together, they would hunt these animals and use the meat for food. Now he was so comfortable in the woods that he could go out on his own, but he still enjoyed his father's company. When his father could not go, he would go over to George's house to see if he could go hunting with him.

Gus learned to shoot a musket back east when he was ten. The musket was almost as big as he was then. He had grown a lot since, and was now able to fire and load his musket with ease. He was a good shot, even when the bird, like a grouse or pheasant began to fly. Somehow, he just had a special ability when it came to shooting. His father told him he had a "good eye." He was also very good at following animal tracks and looking for signs that something had passed by in front of him. Aside from his ability to track animals, Gus also trapped beaver and raccoon for their fur. He was able to sell these at the general store and trading post in Bedford.

There was a wide variety of fish in the stream that ran through the eastern part of their farm and Gus would go there often to catch fish for dinner. It seemed like Gus was more comfortable in the woods or working on the farm than doing anything else he could imagine. He loved nature and being outdoors.

Gus and his parents seemed to be always busy, but the busiest times of the year were the spring and fall. Gus had been working with his parents full-time now for four years since he stopped going to school. He was big and strong enough to plow and drive the team of horses. He could shuck corn almost as quickly as his father and together they seemed to be able to take care of any problem that came up on the farm.

One morning Gus and his father worked together clearing more land. They cut down a tree with a two man saw and chopped the tree up into logs that they would use in the cabin for cooking and heating. By the time the logs were stored in the wood pile beside the cabin, the morning was over and it was time to stop for lunch. His father said he was going back out to the field after lunch to burn the stump so that it would be easier to remove when they plowed the ground next spring for the first time. This did not require two people, so Gus asked, "Could I go fishin' for dinner this afternoon?"

His father replied, "Finish all of your chores and weed the vegetable garden, then you can go."

Gus calculated that it would take him a few hours to do as he had been instructed so he got busy right away so that he could have more time at the stream. Gus hurriedly feed the pigs and chickens and went on to hoe and pull weeds out of the garden. It took him until nearly mid afternoon to finish all the chores. He didn't mind doing the weeding, because sometimes when he pulled out a weed, some dirt would stay attached to the roots and on occasion, in that dirt he would be fortunate enough to find a worm that would be ideal to use for fishing. And that is exactly what happened this afternoon. Gus had four worms in his pocket just waiting to serve as bait for a nice big trout. When he was all done, he returned the hoe to the barn and then went into the cabin and told his mother he had finished his chores and was going to the stream to fish. She handed him a napkin that had a few biscuits and pieces of salted ham in it for him to eat for a snack while he fished.

"Catch us some big ones," she said.

"I will," he promised and grabbed his fishing pole that he kept in one corner of the cabin and hurried out the door, back into the sunlight. It felt warm on his body and he realized how much he liked being outside. He was soon lost in thought and began to whistle as he made his way across the field to the small creek. He had a favorite place where he and his father often went and that is where he was going today.

When Gus got to the creek, he took off his shoes and socks and stuck his feet in the cool water. From this spot, he could lean back against a large tree and relax as the worms invited the trout to swallow his hook. The creek was still running pretty high from the spring rains. He noticed that the baby ducks were getting bigger as they waddled after their mother and hopped into the water in an effort to get away from him unharmed. As Gus settled in, a mocking bird sang all his neighbors' songs and a yellow butterfly moved from one plant to another, never staying in one place very long. Gus marveled at how delicate its wings were. He had a great appreciation for nature and was happy to enjoy it and be a small part of it. Growing up on a farm helped him appreciate all of life. He never took it for granted.

It did not take too long until his line tightened and Gus gave his pole a yank. The fish nibbling at the other end was soon pulled out of the creek and Gus tied a string through its gills and out its mouth so that it did not die until he was ready to take it home. It was a rainbow trout, one of Gus' favorites. He tied the end of the string to his belt and put the fish back into the stream. Gus waited longer for the next strike, but his patience paid off. As his line grew tight, once again Gus gave it a quick yank and the fish that was enjoying a worm meal was soon plucked from the water and it, too, was strung up with the first. Gus enjoyed the challenge of catching the fish and so he was patient. He would thread the worm firmly with the hook, making sure that some was hanging off the ends, and cast it into the stream. He would slowly move the line back and forth or pull it up or perhaps even drawn it back toward himself. The idea was to attract the attention of a big old trout. It did, and this time the fish took a big bite and began to quickly swim away. Gus was not ready and the quick jerk on the line almost caused him to lose his grip on the fishing pole. He laughed at himself as he pulled in the third trout and tied it to the line of fish he had already caught. After he had baited his hook with the last worm, Gus cast out his line one more time and began to move it slowly once again. He thought he heard something and paused to listen, but it was not the dinner bell and it was not his father calling to him. It must have been a bird. He listened for a minute or so, but heard nothing, so he resumed fishing. It took a long time before he finally got a nibble. Gus was wondering if he had caught all the fish that had been living in the stream, but he reasoned that it would be impossible to catch them all in one afternoon. As his line tightened, Gus gave it a jerk once more and out of the water came a fourth fish. This one was a bass. As he looked at his fish, Gus decided that four nice sized fish would make a fine dinner. He would take them home and clean them. His mother would fry them in the big black skillet along with some potatoes. She had made some corn bread for lunch. Maybe there would be some left for dinner. As he looked at his catch, he reasoned that his mother would only eat one and he could split the rest with his father. So, Gus pulled out his line, pulled on his socks and shoes and began to make his way back home. He carried the string of fish in one hand and his fishing pole in the other. The fish that were struggling on the line seemed to be trying to swim away as they wiggled back and forth in an effort to escape. But Gus hung on tightly as he followed the path that led to his home.

Gus was retracing his steps from a few hours earlier when he sensed that something was not right. The team of horses was in the field where his father had been working, but his father was not with them. Nor was he by the stump that he had been burning. He hadn't heard the dinner bell ring and it wasn't that late in the day. Besides, his father would not leave the horses out there unless there was some emergency. Gus looked up at the sky and decided that it was only late afternoon. Since he still had the fish, his mother had not cooked dinner yet. When he looked over at the cabin, he noticed that the front door was open and there seemed to be no activity, no life. He began to look from one familiar place to another in search of his parents. His mother was not in the garden. He didn't see his father near the barn or in any of the pens. Suddenly, Gus had the dreadful thought that perhaps his parents had been killed like the Leininger family at Penns creek. He dropped his fish and pole and ran as fast as he could to the house, calling for his mother as he ran. When he got to the front door, his fears were confirmed. Both of his parents lay dead on the floor. It appeared as if someone had come to the house and attacked his mother. She was lying over in the corner away from the wood stove with the butcher knife still in her hand. His father lay not far from the front door with a wound in his chest. Both of them had been scalped. Their blood stained the floor of the little cabin where they lay. Gus became ill as he looked from one parent to another and as he was vomiting his lunch, he vowed to avenge their death or lose his own life trying. Tears began to pour from his eyes. He could only imagine what must have happened to them and the more he imagined, the more he cried for them and for himself.

After a few moments, Gus pulled himself together and began to think about what he should do. He suddenly realized that his own life could be in danger and he looked behind the door for his musket. It was still there. He had to step over his father's body and move it with the door to get the musket, the powder horn and the leather bag of balls and paper. This he did as gently as he could. He did not want to disturb his father's dead body. The thought seemed strange but somehow it also made sense. He stayed inside the cabin just long enough to load the musket and then carefully looked out the door to see if any Indians were still nearby. Seeing none, Gus began to run as quickly as he could to his neighbors. He was going to cut through the woods, but decided to stay on the path so that he could see if he were about to be attacked. When he got close to the neighbors' house Gus shouted out as he ran, "Mrs. Gillian are you there? Mrs. Gillian?"

Mrs. Gillian opened the door and looked out at Gus. She knew instantly that something was wrong.

"What is it Gus? What's happened?" she asked.

"I was fishin' and came home and found my Ma and Pa both dead and scalped, lying in the cabin." said Gus. "After I looked around a minute, I grabbed my musket and ran over here. You better warn your family. These Indians could be anywhere nearby waiting to kill someone else."

Mrs. Gillian ran to the pole that the bell was mounted on and pulled hard on the bell rope. She rang it over and over to call her husband and children into the house. When they had all come running, Gus told them what he had found at his cabin less than half an hour before. Mr. Gillian got his musket and he and Gus went to another neighbor to tell them the horrifying news while Mrs. Gillian and the family locked themselves in the cabin. Soon Gus, Mr. Gillian and the neighbors returned and the men all made their way back to Gus' cabin. Gus decided he better warn George and his family too, so he and one of the men ran through the woods to the Greer's house where Gus repeated the story one more time. George, his parents and two younger brothers all came back with Gus to his cabin. Two of the men who had come earlier found some wood in the barn and began to use Gus' father's saw to build coffins while the others began to searched the woods around the farm to make sure there were no more Indians lurking nearby. Finding none, they relaxed a bit and returned to Gus' cabin. There were no signs of an attack on the cabin, no arrows or holes from musket balls. The men decided that the Indians must have surprised Gus' mother while she was beginning to prepare dinner. Since his father was near the door, they thought that perhaps he had tried to rescue his wife when he saw the Indians go into the cabin. No one knew for sure, but since both were stabbed and scalped, they all agreed with Mr. Greer when he said, "It looks like the Indians must have snuck into the cabin and killed Katherine and then Albert when he came to her rescue." After their investigation, the men who had been looking for Indians and examining the cabin began to dig two graves in a shaded area behind the cabin. Before they were through, some other neighbors had joined them. Gus' aunt and uncle who lived in Bedford got the news quickly and they, too, came to join those who had gathered to bury Gus' parents.

The men digging the graves and the men building the coffins ended their work at about the same time. With as much dignity as they could, the men lifted Gus' parents one at a time and put them in the coffins they had just made. There was no attempt to change their clothes or make them look any better. They nailed the lids on the top of the coffins and carried them to the holes the other men had dug. When everyone had gathered around, Mr. Gillian said a few nice words about Gus' parents and another man led the group gathered in repeating the 23rd Psalm. Gus got the family Bible and read some of the passages his mother liked to read and also one his father liked about Heaven having many mansions. He was sure that his parent's souls were in Heaven.

They were good people, faithful people. He prayed that God would now look after them.

After they buried his parents, Gus went back to his cabin just long enough to gather up his own clothes and some personal items. As he looked around the little cabin that had been his home, he felt anger and at the same time disbelief. He glanced out the doorway expecting to see his father out in the fields. How could this have happened? What was in store for him now? He did not know for sure, but he was more convinced than ever that he would one day avenge his parent's death. How and when he did not know, but he was sure it would happen. He would make it happen.

After one last look at the cabin that had been his home, Gus went off to Bedford to live with his uncle and aunt who owned a tavern there. As much as he loved the farm, he never wanted to see the cabin and the images it contained again. When Gus got settled into a small room his uncle had been using for dry goods storage, his uncle went back to the cabin to clean the floor and gather up food, cooking utensils, and anything else he thought he could use at the tavern. The rest of the household items he could not use were either sold or stored for Gus to use when he had his own home. Several of the neighbors took the clothes that did not fit his aunt or uncle. After several weeks, the cabin was cleaned out and the animals were also sold to some of the neighbors or the butcher in town. Finally, Mr. Gillian made an agreement with Gus to buy the farm by paying him five dollars month. Gus's uncle would collect the money and save it for him until Gus became of age to start his own family. With that transaction complete, one chapter of Gus' life was over and a new one was beginning.

CHAPTER THREE

Six Indian warriors had run through the woods carrying a smoked ham, two chickens and two bloody scalps. They were led by Tamany and his younger brother Glikikan, the two oldest sons of a Delaware chief. The Indians had found a farm and killed the people there who were working the land. The woman was brave, but not strong enough to take on three of the men at the same time. They snuck into the little cabin while she was preparing dinner. She was not facing the door as they walked right in. They would have taken her with them, but when she saw them she turned around with a knife in her hand and began to swing wildly at them while she screamed. She was able to cut Tamany, but that was the last thing she did. After being cut on his cheek, Tamany stabbed Katherine and then hit her on the head with his tomahawk. That blow knocked her to the ground. Her husband came running from the fields were he was working when he heard her scream. Glikikan, who was standing closest to the door, heard him coming and waited until he entered the cabin. He took his knife out of the sheath that hung around his neck and stabbed the man in the chest as he stepped through the cabin door. The man fell to the floor and moaned as his eyes searched the cabin for his wife. As he lay there, the Indian who had killed his wife bent over her and grabbed her by the hair while cutting it off with his knife. The wounded man could only cry as he watched. In the next instant, Glikikan pulled the knife out of his chest, pulled his head back and cut his throat. Then he grabbed his hair with one hand and cut through his scalp with the knife. The man laid there for a few seconds, realizing he was dying and that his wife was dead. He could do nothing but bleed and pray that his son would somehow be spared. He died hearing the whoops of Indians who had bested their enemy mingled in with his prayer for his son.

The three other Indians were searching the farm for anything they could carry. They found the smoked ham and chased down a few of the chickens. After they saw the man run to the cabin, they too ran there to make sure he did no harm to their friends, two of whom were brothers, the sons of their chief.

With the two white people dead and having stolen the food they wanted, the Indians slipped back into the woods and began to search for another unsuspecting farmer to kill. Maybe they could find captives to take back to their village to be used as slaves or traded away to another tribe. As they made their way through the woods, the two who had killed the white people told the others what they had done. They recounted every detail of the attack and conquest. The scalps would be proof of their bravery when they got back home. The sons of the chief knew their father would be proud. The others also had scalps to show from other conquests when they returned back over the mountains to their home.

Their jubilant mood was broken when the Indians heard a bell ringing. They had heard this before around the villages and forts. They suddenly realized that, somehow, they had been seen or someone had come upon the people in the cabin and the alarm had sounded. Without knowing how many white people were nearby, they decided that the best thing to do would be to run away from the farm toward the mountains and westward toward home.

CHAPTER FOUR

After the raid at Gus' parents' farm, many of the farmers began to work in groups and some of them spent their nights inside the walls of Fort Bedford. That simply meant there were more people than usual in the village going to and from the fort. The village itself was not very large and with the additional people, the conditions were crowded. The tavern where Gus lived with his uncle and aunt was always full of travelers. Gus spent many hours helping with the various chores there. He had to stock the pantry, clean the tables, and take care of the animals of the travelers in the barn. Sometimes Gus thought that feeding the animals and cleaning their stalls was preferable to doing the same for the people. He did not like crowded conditions. In spite of the terrible things that were happening with the Indians, he preferred to be outside in the wide open spaces.

Fort Bedford was large enough to house quite a large number of soldiers along with their supplies and animals. It was not full at the moment, but even those who were there seemed to add to the congestion. The fort was shaped like an irregular pentagon. There were storehouses inside that were large enough to hold three months' worth of supplies. One of the storehouses held provisions and ammunition. The fort was big with picketed log walls, a large ditch outside and a bastion at the five corners where the cannon were mounted. Surrounding the fort were four large earthen ramparts where soldiers could camp and sleep if they did not want to stay inside. And there were also two hospitals and two sutler's buildings that were located just outside the fort. Then there was a store that was a trading post and general store where everyone bought the supplies they needed. A blacksmith had his shop not far from the tavern and it seemed like he hammered horse shoes or metal bands all day long. There seemed to be a steady stream of travelers who would stay at the tavern. That was good for business, but Gus needed some quiet time outside and away from everyone. No, he did not like living in the village at all. It was far too busy and noisy. He missed his parents and the farm life he enjoyed so much.

"The only good thing about Bedford," Gus told George one day when George came to visit, "is the Juniata River that runs right through town, not far from the fort, where I can go to fish. And the fishin' is pretty good. There are perch, bass and trout in the river. I even caught a catfish once, but I threw it back. There is something about their face that just gives me the heebie-jeebies".

He and George went there after his work was done that day and they both enjoyed catching trout and perch which they took back to the tavern and fried up for dinner. Gus was sure the fish tasted better than the stew his aunt had prepared for the guests' dinner. But her cornbread was pretty good and so was her chocolate cake. He and George added these items to their plates when the fish was ready. In spite of what happened to his parents, Gus never thought that not fishing that day would have saved them from their attack. In fact, he still enjoyed fishing very much. It afforded him some quiet time and a chance to be alone.

As time went by, Gus discovered that there was a second good thing about living in Bedford. He met a girl who seemed very nice. She lived down the street from the tavern and Gus would see her at the trading post store. One day, Gus decided that he was going to say hello. So, he walked up to her as she was leaving the store.

"Hello." He said, "My name is Gus."

She looked a little surprised but replied, "Hello Gus, my name is Elizabeth."

"That's a nice name," said Gus. "It suites you. You look like an Elizabeth."

"What does that mean?"

"Well, Elizabeth seems like a sophisticated name and you look sophisticated."

"I'll take that as a compliment and thank you for it," replied Elizabeth. "Is Gus your real name or a nick name?"

"Oh, a nick name," said Gus. "My real name is Gustave. I live with my aunt and uncle at the tavern there."

"Oh," said Elizabeth. "I live just down the street in the small house on the corner."

"Yes, I know," said Gus. "I've seen you coming and going. You just moved here didn't you?"

"Yes," replied Elizabeth. "We came west from Philadelphia to start a congregation here."

"To start a what?" asked Gus.

"A congregation," repeated Elizabeth. "My father is a Presbyterian minister and he came here to start a new church."

"That's nice," said Gus. "We don't have any churches around here. I used to go to church when I was younger before we moved out here."

"Where did you come from?" Elizabeth asked.

"We had a farm just west of Philadelphia but sold it and came out here to start over again." explained Gus.

"If your parents own a farm, why are you living at the tavern?" Elizabeth asked.

"My parents were killed by Indians at our farm a few months back and my aunt and uncle own the tavern. We moved here to live near them. My uncle is, was, my father's brother. That's why I am staying with them." explained Gus.

"I am so sorry to hear about your parents Gustave. Were you hurt by the Indians?" asked Elizabeth.

"No. I was fishin' and came home to find them both dead and scalped." said Gus.

"Scalped!" cried Elizabeth. "How dreadful that must have been!"

"Yes, it was." said Gus. "I'll never forget what I saw when I came into the cabin."

Elizabeth looked at him with great sympathy and put her hand on his arm. Then she said, "I am so sorry for your loss Gus. If you ever need to talk to someone, you feel free to come to see me."

And with that first conversation, a relationship began between two young people.

It didn't take long for Gus to be smitten with Elizabeth. She was so kind and lady-like. The way she moved, the way she walked, the way she looked, the softness of her skin all said "This is a woman." Some times when she looked at Gus, he melted inside. He found himself looking for her often. He even started attending services at the Presbyterian Church in town just to see her. She had this funny way of twisting her finger in her curly hair when she was deep in thought or listening intently. The feelings he had for her were unlike any he had ever had for anyone. He wondered if there was something wrong with him. Sometimes while Elizabeth's father was preaching a sermon, he would just watch Elizabeth instead of listening. In fact, most often he left the service without knowing what was said at all. But he could recall all day long what Elizabeth wore, what she did and how she did it. He would go out of his way to see her and make up excuses to walk by her house. Sometimes he would stand outside her house under the elm tree and listen to her practice playing the piano or singing while her mother played. On the one hand, Gus wanted to be with Elizabeth as often as possible and on the other hand, he felt rather foolish to be following this urge to see her or be near her. When he thought it all through, he figured that he must be in love. It was a new feeling for him, but what else could make a fella act so foolish?

When they had opportunities to be alone together, Gus and Elizabeth talked a lot about themselves and each other and future plans. Gus' only plan for the future was to become a farmer once he could buy a farm again, and to find a way to avenge his parents' death. Elizabeth was much more refined than Gus. She played the piano and sang like a song bird. Since her father was the Presbyterian minister in Bedford, that made him one of the most educated men in the whole region. Her mother gave piano lessons and played for their church services. Elizabeth thought she might like to be a teacher. She was a good reader and enjoyed reading books of poetry. The words sounded nice to Gus, but they did not always make sense. But he would sit and listen to Elizabeth as she read.

The more Gus and Elizabeth saw of each other, the more fond they grew of each other and the more comfortable they felt talking about nearly anything. It was clear that they had come from two different backgrounds and had aspirations that were worlds apart, but they also cared deeply for each other and they both thought that would be enough to see them through any difficult times they might encounter from their backgrounds or aspirations. Neither one of them could see any problem with them both living out their dreams.

It must have become apparent to other people how Gus and Elizabeth felt, because, one day in the spring, almost nine months after his parents died, Elizabeth's father, Rev. McGregor, told Gus that he would like to have a talk with him. Gus agreed and he came to the McGregor house at the appointed time. When he got there they went into a small room that had a book case in it. The pastor called the room his "study".

Rev. McGregor asked Gus, "What do you plan do to with yourself when you grow older?"

Gus replied, "I don't know. Maybe I'll buy some land and become a farmer like my Pa. Or maybe, I'll learn a trade. I'm saving the money that Mr. Gillian is paying me for the farm. When I am old enough, I'll have enough saved to begin to make payments myself."

"Have you thought about a profession such as law, religion, education or medicine?" asked Rev. McGregor.

"No." replied Gus, "I only went to school for six grades and that's plenty for me."

Rev. McGregor said, "Gus, I like you and I think my daughter does as well, but her mother and I had hoped that she would find someone who was a little more sophisticated; someone who was interested in education, religion or the arts."

Gus was stunned. He didn't know what to say. He felt like someone had punched him in the stomach. Finally he replied, "Does this mean you do not want me to see Elizabeth anymore?"

"Yes." said Rev. McGregor, "I believe it would be best if you did not call on her or associate with her more than necessary. That way, she will be able to meet more suitable young men. You do understand don't you, Gus?" he asked.

"Yes," Gus replied. He understood. He was not good enough, maybe not smart enough and certainly not cultured enough for the good Reverend.

As Gus left Elizabeth's house he made a second promise to himself. Just as he promised to avenge his parent's death, now he promised that he would show the good Reverend that he was a good person and not only that, he was good enough for his daughter. Gus was determined to make something of himself to prove to Rev. McGregor that he was able to take care of Elizabeth, to provide for her, even if he did not like the fancy things in life.

Unfortunately Gus was not interested in becoming a teacher or a preacher like Rev. McGregor. In fact Gus was baptized Lutheran, and that probably created more problems since Rev. McGregor was Presbyterian and, for some reason, it seemed to be a concern for adults. But he did love Elizabeth and knew that she loved him too. What could he do? He had no answer right away, but was determined to do something that would change Reverend McGregor's mind.

CHAPTER FIVE

Gus was spending all of his free time trying to make some sense of what was happening in his world. He was a good person. He was a smart person. He worked hard and was honest. But just now, he felt lost. He did not know where to turn to find the answers to the many questions running through his mind.

One day, as he was fishing along the river on the north side of the fort, deep in thought, trying to come up with answers to some of his questions, Gus met an old frontiersman. He too had a fishing pole and was walking along the river looking for a good place to settle down and catch some fish for dinner. When he saw Gus he called out, "Hello there young fella."

"Hello." Gus replied.

The Frontiersman asked, "Are the fish biting?"

"Yes," replied Gus, "I'm using worms. You can have some if you want."

"Thanks," replied the older man. "John Good is my name. Who might you be?"

"I'm Gus, Gus Giron. My uncle owns the tavern in town."

"Oh yes," Mr. Good replied. "I heard tell of what happened to your folks. Sorry boy."

Gus did not reply, but just looked into the water as if the answers to his questions were somehow just under the surface for him to see.

Mr. Good sat down not far from Gus, baited his hook and cast out into the river a short distance away.

Finally Gus asked, "Mr. Good, have you lived on the frontier for a long time?"

"Yes," he replied. "I've been a trapper and trader for many years. Why?"

"Well," said Gus, "I've been trying to make some sense of what's going on with the Indians. We never used to live in fear for our lives, but all I've been hearing is story after story of attacks, killings and people being taken captive. I don't understand what changed."

"Oh," said Mr. Good. "The answer is not an easy one. I suppose you have to know a bit about what has happened to the Indians to be able to understand what is happening now."

"Can you tell me?" asked Gus.

"Well, let me see. Where to begin? For starters, when we white folks came we pushed the Indians away from the coast and cheated them out of land. That wasn't a very good beginning. The Indians moved west, north or south to get away from us. The Delaware are an example. They used to live along the Delaware River east of here. They called the area, "the place where there are forks in the stream", but there is a town there now. It's called Easton. Have you ever heard tell of William Penn?"

"Yes, he owned the whole colony of Pennsylvania." replied Gus.

"Yes, that's right." said Mr. Good. "Well, after he died, his sons bought the property where Easton is now from the Delaware. I can't say for sure, but the story goes that Thomas Penn wanted the land there along the Delaware River and tricked Chief Nutimus into believing that a previous chief had signed a treaty with his father. He called it the "walking purchase". Thomas Penn told the chief that the deal was the Indians would sell the land as far as a man could walk in a day and half. Then he had a track cleared in a straight line and hired the fastest runner in the area to run along the path for a day and a half. I believe the fella's name was Edward Marshall."

"You mean he cheated?" asked Gus.

"Yes, I guess he did. And the Delaware living there were really angry. They asked the Iroquois for help, but got none and were sent packing. They ended up moving west; some as far west as the Ohio Territory over those mountains there.

"Next, for some reason, the British, French, and various Indian tribes all claimed the land west of the Allegheny Mountains into the Ohio Valley. When we trappers and traders began dealing with the Indians, and the Mingo, Delaware and Shawnee began to defy their authority, the French decided to use force to enforce their claims to the Ohio Territory. They turned first to the Detroit tribes for help. The Wyandot, Ottawa, Potawatomi, and Ojibwe, usually were their most dependable allies, but these tribes were thinking of trading with us and the British and did not want to fight the Ohio tribes. The French prevailed upon them and eventually got their support. I believe it was in the summer of 1752 that a mixed blood named Charles Langlade, led a war party of 250 Ojibwe and Ottawa from Mackinac and destroyed the Miami Indian village and British trading post at Piqua, in the Ohio territory. After that, the tribes of the French alliance fell into place like baby ducks following their mama, and the French began to build a line of forts across western Pennsylvania to block our access to Ohio. Most Delaware and Shawnee had no desire to be controlled by the French and turned to the Iroquois for help. Now, to the Iroquois, the French and British seemed like two thieves fighting over their land but they decided the French were the more immediate threat. So, they signed the Logstown Treaty reconfirming their 1744 cessions and giving the British permission to build a blockhouse at the spot where the Ohio River begins. But, before it was finished, the French burned it.

"About ten years after that, a meeting was held up in Albany, in New York, between the colonies and Iroquois to prepare for war with the French. Since they were unable to defend Ohio, the Iroquois ceded it to Pennsylvania, but I believe they wanted to keep the Wyoming and Susquehanna Valleys. Unfortunately, an Albany trader, not me, mind you, managed to get some of the Iroquois representatives drunk on corn whiskey, and when they sobered up, they discovered they had signed an agreement with a Connecticut land company opening the Susquehanna and Wyoming Valleys to settlement. The conference ended with the Iroquois angry at the British about this treaty, Pennsylvania protesting Connecticut's attempt to claim its territory, and the Delaware threatening to kill any whites who tried to settle in the Wyoming Valley. Yes sir, Gus. It was a mess."

"So, we whites tricked them again?" said Gus.

"Well, yes. The Ohio tribes learned that the Iroquois had ceded Ohio at Albany, and they saw another betrayal like the "Walking Purchase" from here in Pennsylvania. Even the Iroquois half-kings whom they had selected to serve with the Delaware, Mingo and Shawnee chiefs joined their revolt and declared that Ohio belonged to the tribes which lived there. Deciding that the British were as much their enemies as the French, the Delaware and Shawnee chose to remain neutral and wait to see what was going to happen.

"Things were not going very well. Some tribes were dead set against any settlement. Others did not seem to mind. Some would trade with the likes of me, while the Ohio tribes seemed inclined to favor the French. After the outbreak of the French and Indian War, back in '55, the Munsee attacked the Moravian mission at Bethlehem massacring eleven missionaries. When the Susquehanna Delaware joined the fighting, all hell broke loose. Ignoring the Iroquois orders for them to stop, 300 eastern Delaware warriors combined with 700 of their relatives from the Ohio, spread death and destruction on the frontier here in Pennsylvania, as well as New Jersey and New York. In November of 55, the Indians massacred some Moravian missionaries at Gnadenhutten while a relief force from Easton was camped over night just six miles away and arrived the next day too late to save them. That next spring, Pennsylvania declared war on the Delaware Indians and offered bounties for scalps and prisoners. New Jersey did the same. I am here to tell you that I got my share of those. They pay better than beaver pelts! That's when that line of forts and blockhouses was built to protect the settlements. Benjamin Franklin was the man in charge of safety for the colony and he established a militia and encouraged the line of block houses as a way of protecting the frontier.

"Some of the eastern Delaware under Teedyuscung got tired of the war and made peace with Governor Robert Morris at Easton, in August of '56. A second peace conference was held at Easton a few months later. This one gave money to the Munsee and Pompton for lands taken by New Jersey without payment, paid the Delaware for land they owned in New Jersey, put together a reservation at Brotherton, and most importantly for the Delaware in the west, Pennsylvania renounced its claim to the lands west of the Appalachian Mountains, which had been ceded by the Iroquois at Albany in 1754. A few years later, a major treaty was signed in Easton once again by twenty three chiefs, Governor Denny from Pennsylvania, Governor Bernard from New Jersey, and the British Indian Agent, George Croghan.

"As you might figure, Gus, the news of the agreement immediately reached Ohio, and the Delaware and Shawnee offered no resistance when the British began to move westward against the French."

"That still does not explain what has happened lately." protested Gus. "The Indians were at peace, then, they suddenly changed. What happened? That's why we moved out here. My parents thought it would be safe."

"Well, Gus, as his soldiers occupied French forts in the Great Lakes area and Ohio Valley, Lord Jeffrey Amherst, the British commander in North America, the pompous fool, decided the former French allies were to be treated like a conquered people. Ignoring the advice of William Johnson, General Amherst ended the practice of annual gifts to treaty chiefs, raised prices on trade goods, and restricted their supply. By 1761 the Seneca were passing a war belt calling for an uprising, but only the Delaware and

Shawnee responded. Johnson found out about the plot during a meeting at Detroit with the tribes of the old French alliance. The unrest continued, and other belts were circulated by the Illinois and the Caughnawaga. However, it took a religious movement to unite the tribes against the British. This came from the Delaware Prophet, Neolin. The Indians called him the "Enlightened". The British referred to him as the "Impostor." From his village near the Ohio River, Neolin urged the rejection of the white man's trade goods, especially rum, and a return to traditional native culture and values. His teachings gained a large following among the Delaware, but his most important convert was Pontiac, the Ottawa chief at Detroit. I've been told that he is trying to unite the tribes to try to stop we white settlers from moving into the Ohio Territory.

"I made my way back east for a little protection and that's why I'm camped out here near the fort."

"Well, now I know why the Indians have been so angry. I guess I still don't understand why they killed my mother and father. I may never know. But I plan to get my revenge as soon as I figure out a way." said Gus.

"Be careful with revenge boy. If we all followed the 'eye for an eye and tooth for a tooth' motto, we would end up with a lot of blind toothless people!" Then he grinned and Gus could see that Mr. Good had a few teeth missing in the front of his mouth.

CHAPTER SIX

Chief Natawatwees was a Delaware Indian chief. Because Natawatwees belonged to the important Unami, or Turtle division of the tribe, he became head chief of the entire tribe. Committed to him were all the tokens of contracts, such a wampum belts, and obligatory writings, including the signed manual of William Penn and other documents down to the time that he and his people were forced to leave Pennsylvania and retire west of the mountains to Ohio, where they settled along the Cayuga River. Natawatwees and his wife had three sons. They were Tamany, Glikikan and the youngest son, Newate.

Newate spent his days like most of the others boys, hunting with both a bow he had made and a musket that had been given to his father by a Frenchmen in trade for beaver pelts. He also liked to fish. Newate had a spear that he used as he stood in the river and waited for the fish to come by. Some of the other boys teased him about how still he could stand just waiting for the right moment to spear a fish. They used a pole with a hook made out of a bird claw to catch fish, but Newate liked the old-fashioned way of his people.

Since Newate was the youngest in his family, he seemed to get special attention from his mother. He thought she was over protective. When he was going out with his brothers or the other warriors, she would always tell them to be sure to bring him back safely. It was embarrassing, and the older brothers teased him about it while at the same time making sure they did what they were told. In spite of the fact that these older brothers had already established themselves as brave warriors having killed whites and Indian enemies, they still feared the wrath of their mother.

Newate enjoyed his life in the village. Most of the families had round wigwams to live in, but Newate and his family lived in a longhouse. It was a long and narrow bark covered house that his entire family shared, including the elders and those who were married with babies. It had a door on both ends but no other openings. They had plenty of food to eat. Newate and the other males hunted and fished. Deer and bear, plentiful in the area where they lived, were particularly valuable for food, clothing, and tools because of their great size. But lately, the beaver pelt had become popular for trading with the French, so they too were caught along the banks of the streams where they lived. For religious reasons, the hare, wild cat, rattlesnake and wolf were never harmed. The women of the tribe were the farmers and raised the children. Corn was their main crop. Its cultivation freed the tribe from the pressure of having to hunt and gather food for survival. The women and older girls would plant the corn in rows with hills spaced five or six feet apart in both directions. When weeds were hand high, they were cut down and the earth was cultivated around each plant. Successive plantings were made in April, May and June. Newate and all members of the tribe shared the responsibility for scaring off birds from the corn fields, but for religious reasons the birds were never killed. Festivals celebrating the corn planting and harvesting were high points of his year. These were occasions for eating, dancing and story-telling. The whole village would take part in these festivals. Newate loved to hear the stories about the ancient people and how his people were victorious over the white men who were trying to take away his land.

Newate's mother prepared corn in a variety of ways: it was roasted in the coals, crushed and boiled to make a kind of "hominy," ground into flour to make corn meal, and dried for winter use. He liked it best roasted on the coals. Chestnuts were ground into flour, and many fruits were dried for winter use. The Delaware regarded tobacco as almost a sacred plant and grew it for both ceremonial and personal use.

Newate was a good athlete. He and the other men played a game with a stick that had a webbed end made of deer hide. With this stick, they caught and threw a small ball to the other members of their team in an attempt to get it past the opposing players and into a goal. Newate played in the middle of the field the tribe had outlined and was a very fast runner. He was by far the best player in the tribe. He was also quite good at other games the tribe played just for fun.

Besides being strong and a fast runner, he was also quite handsome. He had several tattoos on his arms. One was of a deer to remind him of the first deer he killed with his father's musket. The second was of a wolf, a sacred animal for his people. He wore earrings in both ears and had a Mohawk hair cut that left hair stick straight up only in the middle of his head. His mother had made him leggings and he helped her decorate them with a variety of dies and metal studs. On his feet he wore deer skin moccasins that were quite comfortable.

Many of the elders hoped that one day he would choose their daughter to be his wife. He had not selected a wife yet, but was very fond of a girl he had known all his life. Her name was Unamati. She had a nice smile and they had been close friends for many years. She knew a lot about him and he knew a lot about her. She, too, was quite an athlete. She was the best girl who played the only game that both men and women played together. They made a handsome couple, but Newate was not ready to offer her father beaver pelts for her hand. He felt like he had to prove himself as a warrior first and then gather the pelts he needed.

Life seemed to be good for Newate and his tribe, but that was not entirely true. His tribe, the Delaware, had been on the side of the French in their war with the British. Some of their warriors had been killed over the years, but not too many. They had usually come back from these battles with great tales of how the British would stand in a circle and make perfect targets for even a poor shot. But for some reason, the French had given up the fight and now the British people were no doubt going to keep taking their land just like they had when they first came across the great ocean.

One day Newate's father received a war belt from an Ottawan Chief named Pontiac. He wanted Natawatwees to come to a meeting of many chiefs. Newate asked if he could go along and his father said, "Yes, but it will be a long trip and take us many days to walk there. Do you think you can keep up?"

Newate saw this for what it was: a test.

"Yes," he told his father, "you won't have to worry about me."

Provisions were prepared and Natawatwees and Newate, along with some others, began to make their way to meet with the other chiefs to talk about the British and what they should do.

As they walked along, Newate heard the older men talk about how surprised and angry they were by the defeat of their French allies in the war with the British. When word arrived in their villages that the tribes were expected to turn their loyalty to a new European King, they were unhappy.

One of the men predicted, "The British will soon be building new forts, then more white people will come, just like what happened to our ancestors along the Delaware."

"Yes," replied another. "We got along with the French, but the British traders we have seen have not dealt fairly with us. They walk around with their noses in the air. They think they are better than us. Not one English trader ever took an Indian wife. They treat us like we are not as good as they."

Natawatwees commented that he did not like what he had heard about the English leader.

"This Jeffery Amherst, a British man, said that he would not give gifts to the tribes like the French had for years. He is also going to stop giving us provisions and gun powder. And he wants all trading to take place inside the forts so that the traders won't be able to trade any guns, powder, ammunition or rum."

Everyone agreed that they were insulted by this snub, but also were angry to be denied the expected tools, blankets, guns and liquor.

As they traveled, Natawatwees explained to Newate that Chief Pontiac was an Ottawan. They were one of the tribes of Indians who had sided with the French during the recent war. The Ottawans had two chiefs in each tribe. The first was to govern over the civil affairs of the tribe and the other to lead the warriors. Pontiac was a warrior chief. He lived near Fort Detroit when it fell to the English in November of 1760.

Pontiac had called this meeting of the Ottawas, Chippewas, Hurons, Potawatomi, Sauk, Seneca, Miami, Delaware, Shawnee, and several other tribes found around the lakes. He wanted the tribes to reclaim the forts that were now in the hands of the British with the hopes that the French would then come to their aide and life would be like it had been.

When all of the tribes had gathered, the chiefs met and Pontiac began to explain his concern about the British. Everyone agreed that they did not like the British and they were open to hearing any ideas Pontiac might have about how to make changes. Pontiac explained that he wanted all of the Indians to rise up and retake the forts, sending a message to this new English man that he and his people were not welcome in Indian Territory.

Newate was not able to attend the meetings with the chiefs, but he did see Pontiac and was very much impressed. He had heard about some of his speeches and asked his father to tell him more about what Chief Pontiac was proposing. His father explained that the plan proposed would be for Pontiac to lead his tribe in an attack on Fort Detroit and the other chiefs to attack whatever fort was closest to them with such speed and force that the English would not be prepared.

The chiefs all agreed with Pontiac's plan and as soon as they got back to their own regions each would begin to make preparations for attacking the nearest fort or joining other tribes as they did so.

When Natawatwees returned home to his village, he met with his warriors and explained to them what Pontiac had planned, saying that he and the other chiefs had decided to follow Pontiac. All of his warriors were pleased with this decision. Not one man spoke against it. They all felt that fighting the British was important for their own future. If all the Indians joined together, they reasoned, they may just be able to defeat the British.

At the end of the meeting, Newate asked his father, "Can I go with you to fight the British?"

Natawatwees answered his son's question with one of his own.

"Tell me something son, are you afraid to die?" he asked.

Newate replied, "I have killed deer and know how to use the knife, tomahawk, bow and musket. It is the white man that must be afraid of me!"

Natawatwees laughed and said, "We will see. Your mother will probably make me promise to keep you safe!"

CHAPTER SEVEN

Newate waited for his father to decide if he could go fight for the territory. He was sure that this would be his opportunity to show his mother and older brothers that he was old and brave enough to be considered a man, not just the youngest in his family. Although he had heard that the British used muskets with spears on the end and some of the men dressed in odd clothes and walked to the sounds made by a bladder being squeezed and drums, he was not afraid. Some of the stories he had been told were of men who ran away from battles. Others talked about the British using cannon from on top of the fort walls to kill people. He was not afraid of cannon, forts, or the white soldiers, no matter what they wore or how they sounded. They were moving into his tribe's territory and had to be stopped. He would show them how an Indian could kill ten white men.

Finally, after a few days, Newate could not stand to wait any longer. Other warriors were getting ready to leave the camp, to move off to Fort Pitt. He wanted to go as well. After dinner that evening, Newate asked, "Father, have you decided about me going with you to Fort Pitt?"

Instantly he realized that it was not the right time to ask that question. His mother, who had been working on sewing beads onto a summer shirt, stopped and looked over to where Newate and his father were standing. The look on her face indicated that she did not favor having her youngest involved in fighting the British. But Natawatwees said, "You are strong and old enough to fight. We are fighting for our land and your future in this place. You can come along." Then he added to his wife, "I'll look after him."

Newate ran off to share the news with his friends. Some of them were already preparing to go as well. Not everyone had a musket. Some had bows and arrows, but they all had tomahawks and knives. They were happy to see that Newate was going to join them. What a wonderful adventure it would be to show the British once again who the better warrior was. They all began to brag about how many scalps they would bring home and how many captives they would take.

When Newate returned home, his father told him to pack supplies for the trip. Dried meat, smoked fish, corn bread, and dried fruits could be easily taken along. He could also take his fishing spear to catch fish along the rivers and streams as they made their way to the Fort.

Natawatwees said, "We don't know how long it will take to fight these English soldiers, so we need to be prepared to stay as long as it takes."

Everyone at the village was getting ready for the men to go to Fort Pitt. The women and young children were busy helping to prepare. The old men were giving advice. The warriors were checking supplies and weapons. Most of them had muskets. The French had traded fur for muskets and ammunition and the Indians soon found the value of the musket for accuracy and distance. They hoped that these new weapons would serve them well against the soldiers at the fort.

After Newate had packed his food and supplies, he went over to Unamati's wigwam to tell her good bye. She had not heard that he was going with the other braves and was a bit surprised. She asked, "What do you know about fighting soldiers? Why do you have to go? You might get hurt. Then what will I do?" She had said too much and suddenly looked down at the ground, embarrassed that she had let him know her feelings for him and maybe even future plans.

"Now do not worry about me Unamati. Worry about the soldiers. They will not hurt me, and besides, I'm a fast runner!"

Newate smiled and gave his "friend" a hug. Then he turned and ran as fast as he could just to show her what he meant. He stopped and turned, waved goodbye, and noticed that Unamati was crying. His heart sank for he did not want her to cry. He decided that whatever he, did he better were careful. He did not want to make her cry again. He wanted to come home a hero with many scalps and stories of bravery. But the more he thought about it, the more concerned he became.

As he walked back to his family's longhouse, he realized that his attitude had changed. He was not as confident as he had been. In fact, for the first time, he was a little bit scared of what might lie ahead. Fighting soldiers who were protected by a fort could be dangerous. He had no walls to hide behind. He decided that it may be better to be careful than to be brave. But he still felt like he wanted to go and be a part of the battle that was coming. It was for his future, Unamati's future, and the future of his tribe.

The men loaded their supplies and weapons and made their way out of camp. The younger boys, older men and women who remained behind waved to them and wished them well. As they made their way along the trail, the goodbye wishes faded away. Even the barking of the dogs diminished. All the men could hear was the sounds they made as the walked along single file, their destination known, but their destiny left in the hands of the Great Spirit.

CHAPTER EIGHT

Newate and the other warriors made their way steadily southeastward toward Fort Pitt. Though they lived along the waterways, they did not use their canoes, but walked along well established paths. The Indians had traded freely with the French at the same spot where Fort Pitt now stood and many from this tribe had been to this point where the Ohio was formed.

When the Indians camped for the first night, Newate asked his father how they were going to fight the soldiers in the fort.

Natawatwees replied, "We have not decided yet, but I do not think it wise to try to attack the fort. We should surround it and cut off the supplies the soldiers need. They will be forced to stay inside and we will just wait. We can live off the land. There are plenty of fish and game. But the soldiers will not be able to get out of the fort to get more supplies. We will only attack the fort if necessary."

"Won't the British army try to come to help the soldiers?" asked Newate.

"Yes, I am planning on that. So far, the British have not proven that they are better warriors than the Indians. Most of their leaders are weak and do not plan well for battle. The only times they have won have been when they had many more men and weapons. We will be ready when they come."

Newate considered this and realized that being the chief meant that his father needed to be wise and brave as well as a good leader. He was proud of his father and was ready to go to battle with him when the time came.

The next morning, Newate asked his father if he could go out front with some of the scouts who were leading the main party to the fort. Since they were still a day's walk away from their destination, Natawatwees agreed to let him walk up front next to his oldest brother, Tamany. Newate gathered his bow and supplies and ran to catch up to his brother. As they walked along, Newate asked him to retell the story about how he had been cut by the white lady. He was teasing his brother because he was one of the strongest of the braves and one of the best warriors. When he came back recently from a raiding trip over the mountains, he had a scar on his face. He tried to say that he had gotten it in a fierce fight to the death, but his middle brother who was with him explained that the fight had been with a woman.

About midway through the story as it was being recounted by Tamany, Newate noticed the smell of smoke. He motioned for his brother to be quiet and they both stopped walking and began to sniff the air and listen. In a few seconds, they determined the direction from which the smoke was coming and carefully followed it to a campsite. There was a man cooking breakfast over a small fire. It looked like he was the only person at the site. He must have been a trapper because he had beaver pelts in one pile, fox fur in another, and additional supplies piled up next to him on the ground. The brothers determined that he was not dressed like a Frenchmen and therefore must be a an Englishman. This man was going to die.

Tamany began to aim at the trapper with his musket, but Newate put his hand up and pointed to himself indicating that he wanted to kill the man. His brother nodded and Newate took an arrow from his quiver and slowly drew back on the bow string. He let the arrow fly and it entered the man's body in the middle of his back. The man tried to rise up and turn to defend himself, but Tamany was upon him with his tomahawk raised. He smashed him on the head and the man collapsed to the ground. Newate shouted a war whoop and also ran to the man. In an instant his hair was yanked and scalp cut off. It was the first time Newate had killed a man. After the initial jubilation, as Newate stood and looked at the man he had killed, there was a let-down and he was not so proud of himself. It had not been much of a fight. He simply shot the man in the back. It was little different than shooting a deer standing still.

The war whoop brought others running and soon Natawatwees was standing beside his sons asking what happened. After an explanation was given, Newate was celebrated as a hero. He had killed the first enemy of this campaign. For his bravery, he was able to keep the man's valuable pelts and furs but most importantly, his musket and ammunition.

The warriors spent time that day in celebration and dance in honor of Newate. They prayed that the Great Spirit would continue to keep him safe.

After the celebration and lunch, Natawatwees sent Newate and his brothers back to their village with the pelts taken from the dead man. Newate could use them to trade with the French after he got back from fighting the British or perhaps he could consider using them as a gift for Unamati's father. The supplies the trader was carrying would be used by the rest of the men as they laid siege to the fort. Natawatwees instructed the brothers to hurry back to join them before they got to the fort.

When Newate and his two older brothers entered their village, everyone gathered to see what had happened. The oldest brother with the scar on his face told the story of how Newate had smelled the smoke and killed the trapper. He then displayed the pelts and the scalp. Newate showed them the musket that he took from the dead trapper. The whole village was very proud of the chief's youngest son. Unamati was most proud, well maybe the second most proud. Newate's mother was most proud of her baby boy who had become a man. Unamati beamed as the story was told and was the first one to congratulate Newate with a long hug. Newate blushed because he was a hero and a warrior. Now was not the time for hugs, although it did feel good. As they embraced, he became aroused for the first time with a woman. That made him even more embarrassed and he wondered if Unamati was aware of what had happened as they stood there squeezing their bodies together.

The pelts were stored in the longhouse and the brothers were fed and sent off once again to catch up to the rest of the men. One of the older men promised that he would prepare the scalp and hang it on a pole outside their longhouse. Newate was one of the men now for sure. He was still the youngest, but with his first kill, he was now considered a man and a warrior in the eyes of his tribe.

CHAPTER NINE

After stopping along the trail overnight, Newate and his brothers got up early in the morning and started out to catch up with their father and the other warriors. They began to jog along the trail in an effort to make up time. The oldest brother led the way. He was the strongest of the three. Newate could out-run him in a short race, but not in a long distance run like this. So he was content to run second and try to keep pace.

As they ran, the brothers began to tease Newate about the obvious affection he had for Unamati and hers for him.

Tamany said, "Now that you have all those pelts, you'll probably want to run back home and talk to Unamati's father about your future plans."

Then Glikikan added, "Yes, and when we get back, we're going to have to add on to the long house to make room for the two of you and all the children you will have."

Once again, Newate blushed. He was not so sure about sex. He had never been with a girl in that way. But he did like Unamati and she seemed to like him. Maybe he would talk to his father about this to see what advice he could give.

By alternating jogging and walking, the brothers were able to catch up to the others just before the evening meal. Their tribe had camped just west of the Allegheny River along the banks of the Ohio. The plan was to wait there for some other tribes to join them before they decided how best to attack the fort. They did not want to let the British know they were nearby. Lookouts were posted in all directions to detect any scouting parties from the fort, but none had ventured out when the brothers arrived.

The next day, warriors from the Mingo, Shawnee and Wyandot tribes began to arrive at the camp. James Logon was the leader of the Mingos. He had been raised in Pennsylvania and his father named him after an English friend. The Mingos were a part of the Iroquois Nation who had been forced to move from New York and Pennsylvania by the white settlers and were now living near the Delaware in the eastern part of the Ohio territory. The Shawnee spoke the same language as the Delaware and called the Wyandots their "uncles". Their language was called Algonquian and many tribes spoke some form of it. These tribes were closely related and were preparing a unified front to face the British. They had similar customs and living styles. They were all farmers and hunters, but when pushed, they could be warriors. This was one of those times. They all believed that by taking Fort Pitt, they could keep the British and the settlers east of the mountains. This was going to be the most important siege of their history and to a man, they were determined to win.

When all of the chiefs gathered to plan their next moves, Natawatwees stood before them and said, "I have fought against the white soldiers from England before. I have fought against the white militia from Virginia and Pennsylvania. They do not fight well. Their leaders do not plan well. We can win if we plan well. The fort is a half-day's walk from here on the other side of the river. It is well built. We cannot attack it and overcome the soldiers there. I believe we should not risk lives doing this. But we should surround the fort and keep the soldiers inside. That will make them use up their supplies. If we hear of an army coming to bring the fort supplies, we can attack it as we have so many others and kill the soldiers, keeping the supplies they bring for ourselves. The soldiers will starve to death, or give up, and then we will take them captive or kill them."

James Logon agreed with Natawatwees and suggested that each tribe be responsible for a certain area around the fort. It was determined that the Delaware would take the east side of the fort from the Monongahela River to the Allegheny River. There was a hill there from which they could watch the fort. Any supplies that would come over land from the east would also come from that direction using Forbes road. The Mingo were given the high hillside overlooking the fort from the south across the Monongahela River. The Shawnee and Wyandot were given the flat west side across the Allegheny River. They were also given responsibility of controlling the rivers.

When all had agreed upon the plan, the Indians set out to take on their responsibilities. The Delaware were the first to move out. They had to cross the Allegheny River north of the fort and extend their warriors from the eastern banks of the river all the way over to the northern banks of the Monongahela. This line would cut off communication between the fort and the British leaders east of the mountains. The men quickly made canoes and rafts and carried them to the river bank. It took several hours for all of the Delaware warriors to be ferried across the river. Next came the Mingo's, who needed to cross the Ohio west of the fort to be able to get to their position on the southern banks of the Monongahela. When they were in place, the Shawnee and Wyandot would secure the west bank of the Allegheny and the north bank of the Ohio. This would ensure that no assistance came down from the north and the soldiers could not escape west by boat into the homeland the Indians had just left unprotected.

The plan worked well. Once all the tribes were in place, the Delaware fired their muskets at the fort. The soldiers quickly responded by bringing the people who lived in the small village into the fort, drawing up the draw bridges, closing the gates and returning fire. Then the Mingo showed themselves on the south side and the Shawnee and Wyandot did the same on the west. Again, the soldiers responded by firing back with their muskets and cannon. With each successive tribe showing themselves, it became obvious to the soldiers that they were encircled. They prepared for an attack, but it did not come. The Indians stayed out of range of the cannon and musket and simply camped there, content to watch and wait. Soon the chiefs made their way to the fort and let it be known that they wanted to talk about terms of the soldiers surrendering the fort. Captain Simeon Ecuyer, the fort commander, was not about to negotiate, but he gave them gifts of blankets and a handkerchief as they departed the talks. These items had been used in the fort's smallpox hospital and he was hoping to infect the Indians who had surrounded his fort.

CHAPTER TEN

After a few days, it became clear that the Indians were not going to attack, but wait the soldiers out. Captain Ecuyer decided that he better send for help. He quickly composed a letter to Major-General Jeffery Amherst and asked for two volunteers to try to sneak through the enemy lines during the night. Two brothers, Carl and John Watkins agreed to take on the challenge. They were from Virginia and knew the territory pretty well. When Captain Ecuyer met with them he said, "It is imperative that this message get through. We cannot outlast a siege without supplies and a supply train that does not know of our situation will only be ambushed and new supplies will never get to us in time. The lives of all of us depend upon your getting this message through. Do you think you can do it?"

The brothers looked at each other and then replied, "We can do it."

Fortunately, the night was cloudy and there was only a sliver of moon shining. The brothers decided not to take their muskets, but only their knives. They would have to eat what they could find or kill with their knives as they made their way east. They wore buckskin shirts and pants and smeared wagon axle grease on their faces and hands and slowly lowered themselves over the southern wall of the fort that ran along the Monongahela. Once there, they began to crawl along the ground eastward, parallel to the river, but not on the river bank. They made their way to the place where the Delaware were camped and watched for a few minutes to determine how best to get around these Indians. The Monongahela River ran northwestward from Virginia toward Fort Pitt and the current was pretty strong. They decided that swimming too far would be difficult and probably noisy, but the Indians had a fire burning right on the river bank and the warriors were spread out in a line as far as they could see to their left. The only option seemed to be going quietly into the water and swimming underwater around the camp fire.

Carl made his way to the river first. He took a deep breath that he hoped would not be his last and crawled into the river like a beaver. Once under water, he swam outward toward the middle and away from the camp fire. After thirty seconds or so, he had to come up for air. As his head broke the surface of the water, he tried not to gasp for breath that may alert an Indian on guard. While slowly taking in small breaths, he treaded water and watched as his brother John slithered into the river. Half a minute later, John's head also popped up out of the water not too far from the spot where Carl was waiting for him. Once they had rested a bit, they repeated the underwater swimming against the current to try to get beyond the Indian line. Four times they swam and came up for air, each time moving steadily beyond the camp fire. Finally when the men were nearly exhausted, they made their way back toward the river bank. As soon as their hands touched ground, they eased their way out of the water as carefully as they could, trying not to splash as they pulled themselves up on the muddy banks. They lay there in the shrubs that grew along the river and rested with their chests heaving up and down until they felt like they could begin to crawl once again. On their bellies once more, they made their way along the river bank until they felt like they had safely evaded detection.

After resting once again, the brothers began to crawl into the woods and then to walk away from the Indians. They knew that breaking a twig or stick may bring Indians searching for them and so they had to be careful. Fortunately, the woods were dark and the brothers felt like it would be difficult to see them as they made their way from tree to tree. With every step their confidence grew and their pace picked up. Soon they were running, trying to make sure not to stray too far from the river that they would use as a guide in this portion of their eastward trip.

After several hours of walking and running, the brothers decided to rest. Their clothes were still damp, so they took them off and hung them over bushes to dry. Then they found a soft spot beneath an oak tree and fell asleep, certain that the worst was over.

The brothers awoke the next morning to a sunny day. The bright rays brought warmth to their bodies and lifted their hopes. Within a few minutes of getting dressed once again, they were able to find a small stream and use the water to get a drink. Next to the stream were some back berry bushes that provided fruit for their breakfast. What they wanted was some hot coffee, but they had none and would not have started a fire even if they did. No, the berries would have to be enough for now.

They did not continue to follow the river. Instead, the brothers decided to walk into the direction of the rising sun and to avoid the roads and trails that ran through the woods.

At the end of their first day, Carl decided to try his luck with a fishing spear in the stream they had come across. John gathered some wood and started a small fire. Carl waded into the stream and waited with his spear ready. After a few minutes, a brook trout swam near enough for him to throw the spear, but he missed. Somehow he had forgotten what he had learned as a child about the things under water not being exactly where they seem to be. He was determined that he would not miss again. Maybe it was his hunger that made him too anxious. When he had a second opportunity, he threw the spear and this time came up with a trout squirming on the end of it. John quickly cleaned it and laid it over a Y shaped stick to cook. Within a few minutes, the fish was steaming hot and the brothers each took a half and ate it all but the head, tail and bones. They put out the fire and watched the woods intently to make sure that no one had seen or smelled the smoke. Hearing or seeing no signs of anyone else around, the brothers settled down to rest once more before they traveled on.

The next morning, John climbed a tree as the sun was coming up and he could see mountains off in the distance to the east. When he came down he told Carl, "I saw the mountains. Fort Ligonier is on this side of them, so I think we can get there today if we hurry."

The brothers walked with more determination now and even though they were tired and hungry, they seemed to have renewed energy as they made their way toward the tree covered mountains.

As the sun began to set behind them, the brothers came across a road that they thought would take them to the fort. They followed it, Carl walking on the left side and John on the right in the event someone came along and they would have to hide. But they were fortunate. Within an hour, the outline of the fort appeared. The brothers began to run toward the fort, jumping and shouting. A sentry saw them coming and mistook them for Indians and fired at them. The brothers stopped running and held up their hands. As they did so, they looked at each other and realized that some of the axle grease, along with the mud from crawling along the river bank and several days of walking through the woods made them look more like Indians than white gentlemen. They laughed out loud at their own appearance and called out to the sentry to let them in.

Once inside the fort, the men met with Colonel Burd, the fort commander. They apologized for getting the letter wet that Captain Ecuyer had written, but produced it none-the-less, faded ink and all.

Colonel Burd said, "Alright now tell me everything that happened from the beginning."

The brothers responded by telling him how the Indians had surrounded the fort and their adventure of the past few days. When they were finished, Colonel Burd ordered the cook to prepare them whatever they wanted and then told them to find a place to bunk down for the night. In the morning he wanted them to take some horses and a squad of men to ride over the mountains to Fort Bedford and Fort Carlisle to tell Major-General Amherst what had happened.

The brothers were given new clothes and told to get cleaned up. This they did quickly because they knew that once clean, they would be given something to eat. After enjoying a nice meal, the brothers rested and soon fell asleep on the bunks in the barracks of the fort. The next morning, they were given supplies enough to get to Fort Carlisle and were soon on their way, along with six other men, to pass on the information they hoped would save Fort Pitt and their trapped friends.

The road they took led them over the mountains and, as it leveled off a little, along side the Juniata River that led to Fort Bedford. Upon entering the fort, the Watkins brothers retold the story of the Indian siege of Fort Pitt. Once again, they were fed well and rested over night then were sent off the next day to Fort Carlisle where they would meet Major-General Amherst.

CHAPTER ELEVEN

Colonel Henry Bouquet was born in 1719 in Pays de Vaud, Switzerland. His parents were aristocrats in the leading families. When he was 17, Henry became a cadet in the Swiss Regiment. By 1744 he was a Colonel. During his twenty years of military service, Bouquet had learned about war in the war of Austrian Succession and experienced guerilla warfare in the mountains of northern Italy and the Piedmont. Shortly thereafter he met Benjamin Franklin in France. Dr Franklin was, among many other things, a Colonel in the Pennsylvania militia. As they talked, Franklin told him about the endless possibilities of someone with his talents in the colonies in America and so he decided to go and see what his future may hold.

In 1757, Colonel Bouquet was given the opportunity to serve under the command of General Forbes and in 1764, he was given command of all the British forces in Pennsylvania, Maryland and Virginia. He had been commissioned by the British to help organize and command the first Royal British Regiment recruited from the American colonies. The regiment was called the 60th Regiment of Foot, or Royal Americans, and was made up primarily of Pennsylvania Dutch, English, Irish and Scottish immigrants. Under his command was also the British 42nd Regiment or Royal Regiment, the 77th Regiment, also known as Montgomery's Highlanders, and members of the Black Watch who had recently served in the West Indies under his command.

Colonel Bouquet was given the order by Major-General Jeffery Amherst to put together an army to defeat the Indians that had Fort Pitt under siege. As quickly as possible, he gathered together his Royal British regiment and sent word to Francis Fauquier in Williamsburg asking for assistance from the Virginia militia. The Governor wrote back to Bouquet that a large number of volunteers from the Virginia militia were being discharged so they could join his campaign. Colonel Bouquet was perfect for this group because of his training, his international experience and his ability to communicate with all of these men. They were an odd assortment of men: from German, Scotch, Irish and English backgrounds, all led by a Swiss Colonel in the name of Britain.

Not only was this army a strange mixture of men from different countries and backgrounds, it was also an unusual mixture when it came to how it looked and the weapons they preferred to use. The Highlanders wore kilts, stockings, bright red coats and hats to match. The Virginia militia and the men of the 60th Regiment of Foot wore normal frontier clothes. There were no uniforms. The men simply wore what they had. Some of the men dressed like Gus. Their hand-made clothes and three pointed hats were either brown or black. Their shoes were plain and black. Others wore clothes made of animal skins such as deer. These were the men who lived in the wilderness. Some of these men also wore moccasins like the Indians, while others wore boots or shoes. Though Colonel Bouquet had the provisions to outfit his troops, many of the Pennsylvania Dutch used their own weapons, the Jager musket that was made in Germany and used for hunting. It was a 54 caliber musket with a 28 inch barrel length that weighed about eight pounds. Like all muskets, it was a flintlock that fired when the piece of flint, held in the jaws of a spring-loaded hammer, struck the hardened steel face of the frizzen, knocking the frizzen forward to uncover a small pan of gunpowder beneath it. The resulting spark ignited the powder in the pan and this flame was transferred through a small hole to ignite the main powder charge inside the barrel. The powder that had been placed in the barrel exploded, propelling the ball out the end.

The Highlanders, on the other hand, used the British "Brown Bess". It was a favorite for the British because it was as reliable as any other musket and it was able to have a bayonet attached to the end of the barrel for close combat once the musket had been fired, if necessary. It was also reinforced in the stock so that it could be used as a club. It fired a spherical ball of 14 to the pound and would carry straight for 100 yards, and its effective range was about double that distance. These Highlanders had proven their skills using both the musket and the bayonet. They were brave and rugged men, willing to fight to the death.

Like the men from Pennsylvania, the Virginia militia brought their muskets as well. They looked like a cross between the sturdy German muskets and the stylish English muskets. They were used by men all over the James River Basin area and could be used just as easily to hunt Indians as deer. Many of these men had already been engaged in one or more of the battles fought throughout the French and Indian War that had just ended. Some had been with Washington at Fort Necessity and others with Braddock. They would be a good addition to Bouquet's force of Scottish, Irish, English and Pennsylvania Germans.

A few of the militia also carried small muskets called a blunderbuss to fight in close quarters with the Indians. These men figured that the Indians were not going to line up and fire at them like the British and French had done. So, the blunderbuss was brought along because it could be used almost like a pistol. But it could be filled with a shot of buck or a ball. Once they fired their muskets, it would take nearly thirty seconds to reload them while standing up. If they were in the midst of a close battle, the blunderbuss could serve as a back up weapon.

Bouquet sent out thirty of his fittest men to go ahead to Fort Ligonier, over the mountains in the Laurel Highlands. They would help boost the number of men in this small fort which had not been taken as yet. A whole company was sent to Fort Loudoun as a guard for cattle and horses. Then on July 18, 1764, Colonel Bouquet left Carlisle Pennsylvania with four hundred and fifty men and wagons loaded with barrels of flour for Captain Ecuyer and the troops under siege by the Indians at Fort Pitt. The Highlanders had their drums and pipes to keep the time as they marched along and the men from Pennsylvania and Virginia added drums and fife of their own. It was a strange mixture of men and music that tramped the road and filled the air as Bouquet's army left Carlisle to begin their journey together.

The going was slow. Many of the Highlanders and Black Guard were malaria convalescents from their recent West Indian fighting. They lacked the strength for a quick paced march. In addition, winter storms and spring rains had washed away bridges and the roads were in poor condition. The heavy wagons loaded with food were pulled and pushed along the road by both beast and man, making the march even more tiring for the men who had to help push the wagons up the steep grades and out of the ravines.

After eight days of marching, Colonel Bouquet and his men reached Fort Bedford with fife, pipes and drums announcing their arrival. The last two days were harder than the first six because Bedford was located at the foothills of the mountains that ran from the Carolinas through Pennsylvania. Pushing the wagons out of ravines was easy compared to pulling them up hills and through the streams where their wheels got stuck in the mud. By the time they reached Fort Bedford, the men and horses were tired. They needed a rest. It had been a hard eight days. The post commander, Lieutenant Carre, greeted Bouquet as he entered the gate.

"I trust that you had an uneventful march, sir," said Lieutenant Carre.

"We encountered no resistance, but I realized after we left Fort Carlisle, that we were being watched by Indians." replied Colonel Bouquet. "Some of the members of the Virginia militia had seen them hiding behind the trees and moving along parallel to the column as it marched along the road. Though we lost a few of the Highlanders who were acting as our flankers, I'm not sure that it was due to any Indian activity. There were not enough of them to fear attack to the main party, but it was a bit unsettling."

"I should say so, sir," replied Carre, "but your force was far superior to any of the raiding parties we have been hearing about."

"You are quite right, Lieutenant," replied Bouquet, "but I've decided to commission a detachment of woodsmen from Colonel Cresap at Fort Cumberland as scouts. I have sent off some of the Virginia militia men to get them and bring them here. They should be here tomorrow. I believe I could also use some scouting help from any of the local folks around here who may be interested in signing up. I'll pay them regular militia pay and provisions if they do. The Highlanders are good soldiers, but as I said, I lost several of them on the trip from Carlisle. They seem to have no sense of direction and simply can't be used as flankers. They were constantly going missing instead of doing us any good at all. I believe that I will need all the help I can get if I am to relieve Fort Pitt."

"Yes, sir," replied Lieutenant Carre. "I'll have a notice posted announcing that you seek scouts right away."

"The men and horses are tired from the march. Please make sure they are fed well tonight. We still have a long way to go before we get to Fort Pitt." said Colonel Bouquet

"Yes, sir." replied the Lieutenant. "I will ask the cook to prepare something special for the men, and have the men working in the stables give the animals some extra grain."

"Very well, Lieutenant. Now how about a complete report of supplies on hand as well as any report of Indian activity?" asked the Colonel.

After the reports were given, the post commander and the Colonel were joined by the other officers and Mrs. Carre for dinner. The cook had prepared a stew that was followed by venison, potatoes, green beans and corn bread. The officers were delighted with the meal. Most meals while marching were not so good.

As they ate, Lieutenant Carre remembered the account of Gus' parents being killed the summer past. He was aware of others in more remote areas who had been killed as well, but there had been no attack on the fort or the village as yet. He was certain that the fort could repel any warring Indian raid. Colonel Bouquet reminded him to not be overly confident and to always be prepared.

While Bouquet waited for the scouting party from Cumberland, he and Lieutenant Carre continued their inspection of the fort, the supplies and the troops. Bouquet wanted to make sure all was in order with his men and with those who were left behind to defend the fort.

The next morning, Captain Barrett and his woodsmen scouts arrived from Fort Cumberland along with the men who had been sent to get them. They were greeted by the men from the Virginia and Pennsylvanian militia. In fact, some of the men knew each other from previous encounters against the French. The men from Maryland were given supplies for the rest of the march and preparations were made for the army to begin its advance westward.

Everyone was anxious to begin, but also grateful for a little rest as the reorganization took place.

CHAPTER TWELVE

Since early June, the towns' people and farmers around Fort Bedford began to abandon their homes at night and move into the fort to sleep. The farmers would work in the fields during the day in groups of four, always allowing two men to stand guard. Gus' uncle decided to keep his tavern open because it was close to the fort and if trouble came, they could easily run there. After Colonel Bouquet arrived with his army, the small fort became very crowded. But the additional men gave the people who lived in the area some added confidence.

At the tavern the day after Bouquet arrived, Gus heard men talking about a notice that had been posted on the outside wall of the fort asking for volunteers to sign up as scouts to accompany Colonel Bouquet in his effort to end the siege at Fort Pitt. He went to the fort to see what it said for himself. Indeed, Colonel Bouquet was recruiting local men to join him. There was a promise of payment as well as supplies for all who signed up. Not far from that notice was another that offered rewards for Indian scalps. Gus quickly dismissed the idea of cutting someone's hair off, remembering the sight of his parents as he found them in their log house, but he was excited to see the first notice about the army seeking volunteers. He knew that this was his opportunity. Although he had never killed a man before, he had killed squirrel, rabbit and deer. In fact he had won his musket in a shooting contest just the year before. It was made right there in Pennsylvania by his German immigrant relatives. It was a new style of musket that had rifling in the barrel that enabled it to shoot longer and with more accuracy. It still took a long time to load it and he had to do it standing up, but it was great for hunting. And though scalping was not for him, he would not hesitate to kill one of those Indians who had killed his parents with his new musket or even with his knife if he had to. After all, despite what Mr. Good said, even in the Bible it said "An eye for an eye and a tooth for a tooth." He was going to get his revenge.

After he had read the notice, Gus went into the fort and asked to see the man responsible for recruiting scouts. When he was shown to the man in charge of recruiting, he was asked a few questions.

"What is your name?" asked the recruiter.

Gus replied, "Gus Giron."

"How old are you Gus?" the recruiter asked next.

Gus replied, "I'm sixteen, sir."

"Tell me about your experience as a woodsman." said the recruiter.

"I've lived here for four years and have been hunting and fishing in these parts and west into the mountains. I track well and am a very good shot. In fact, I won this musket in a shooting contest." said Gus.

He showed the man his musket and the recruiter was impressed. The army recruiter thought for a moment and then asked, "What do your parents think about you becoming a scout?"

Gus relied, "My parents were killed in an Indian raid at our farm."

"Oh," replied the recruiter, "I'm sorry; I did not recognize your name. I remember hearing about that. Sign here Gus and welcome. I think you'll be a fine scout."

Gus signed on the paper the recruiter gave him and was as of that moment officially a scout. He was then issued supplies and some money for signing up. Though he had his own hunting knife, he was issued a tomahawk to carry. The idea was that after he fired his musket, he may have to defend himself with this weapon. He would have to practice using it at the fort and as he walked along the roads and trails to Fort Pitt. Unlike the

Highlanders, his musket did not have a bayonet, so once he fired it, he would have to take the time required to reload it. So, having the tomahawk in his belt could indeed save his life. He also got a cartridge box to carry ammunition, a tin canteen to carry water, a linen haversack with a three button flap to carry food and small items, and a knapsack, also made of linen, painted to be water-proof. To these supplies, Gus added an extra pair of shoes and socks, some clothes, a fishing line and hook and candles. He was now ready to go to avenge his parents' death. He had no thoughts of it being easy, but he saw it as an opportunity.

Gus left the fort with his supplies and went to the tavern. He told his aunt and uncle what he had done and gave them the money he had received for signing up. He asked them to save it along with the money from Mr. Gillian was paying each month. Although they both voiced their concern, they knew that Gus had already made up his mind. All they could do was wish him well and pray.

Even though Gus had been asked by Rev. McGregor to not see Elizabeth again, he felt that since they had shared so much, he needed to tell her what he had done. He had not gone to visit her since that day, and he heard through a friend that Rev. McGregor had told his daughter that she was not to see Gus any more. Of course he had seen her in the little town, but he did not try to speak to her or ask her to go for a walk or any of the things he wanted to say or do. Now was different. He had made a decision and he wanted her to know about it. He walked over to the quarters that Elizabeth and her family had been given and up to the door. When he knocked on her door, she answered it. She was a bit surprised to see him, but the smile on her face revealed her true feelings. She quickly stepped out of the door-way into the parade grounds of the fort so that they could talk in private. Gus was not sure what he should say or how he should say it, but he knew he had to tell this woman he cared for more than anyone else what he had decided to do. So he simply said,

"Elizabeth, I've signed up to be a scout with Colonel Bouquet. We leave tomorrow."

Elizabeth turned pale and nearly passed out. Gus caught her before she fell to the ground and then called out for help. His call brought Mrs. McGregor running to see what was wrong. Gus explained what he had done and Mrs. McGregor smiled a bit as she patted her daughter's face and talked to her softly.

"Now," she said, "why would you go and do a thing like that, boy?"

Gus couldn't tell her the truth but hated to lie to her, so he told a half truth.

"I've been hearing the stories from the farmers and others of how the Indians have killed so many people and taken little children." He said. "I thought maybe I could help stop the killing and find those precious little ones. Besides, we can't just stay cooped up in this fort forever."

Elizabeth had recovered from Gus's news and her expression had begun to change into something he had not seen before. She looked angry as she straightened herself up and pointed her outstretched finger right at him.

She said, "Gustave Giron, if you go off hunting Indians and get yourself killed, I'll never speak to you again!"

Gus was dumfounded but then he laughed and said, "If I get killed, you won't be able to!"

"Do you think this is funny?" Elizabeth asked. "You are only sixteen. Let the grown men go fight the Indians!"

"Elizabeth," said Gus, "I am a man, and I am going, and when I'm done, I'll come right back here to see you again even if your..."

Gus stopped there and then he quickly kissed her on the cheek for the first time ever. And as quickly as he could, he turned around, gathered his things and ran back off to the area where the scouts were gathering.

Gus had never kissed a girl before, except for his mother, and that was different. As he ran, he realized that when you love someone you feel strange inside. He wondered if it felt this way all of the time when people were married, or just for a little while. More than ever, Gus was determined to show Rev. McGregor that he was good enough. He hoped he would be and that someday soon he would indeed come back.

Gus reached his destination in just a few minutes and began to look around for the scouts from Maryland. He knew that Fort Bedford had been built by the British when General Forbes was building a new road across Pennsylvania to capture Fort Duquesne. The people who had lived around here told his family that at first, the fort was called the "camp at Raystown", after a trader who lived in the area. But finally, the name was changed to Fort Bedford after the Duke of Bedford. The plan was to build a new fort within about one days march from the last one as they stretched west. The Colonel responsible for its construction was the same man who had just come to the fort with his army that Gus had just signed up to join. The purpose of this fort was to function as a base of operations for the British forces and to be a supply depot. As Gus walked along the side of the fort he noticed, as if for the first time, that the walls of the fort were made of vertical stockade oak logs. The logs had been hewn flat on two sides to fit snugly together. It was shaped like a five pointed star with bastions extending from each corner. The fort had a large ditch around it that was about five feet deep and three feet wide. The dirt that had been dug out of the ditch was piled up against the bottom of the large logs to keep them in place. He had seen the fort many times, but now that he was a part of the army, it all seemed different. He looked at it as if to determine if it was sturdy enough to withstand an attack. On the inside of the fort, there was a six foot wide platform that ran on the inside wall and stood about five foot above the ground. The soldiers could stand on this platform and defend the fort from attackers in any direction. The powder magazine was outside of, but near the fort. And there was one wing of the stockade that ran right down to the river bank. This would afford the soldiers protection as they went to draw water if the fort was under siege. As Gus looked it over, he was amazed at the structure and strength of it. If Fort Pitt was built the same way, he thought, the people there would be safe.

When he finally found the other scouts, Gus introduced himself to the fifteen other men who had volunteered from around Bedford. They soon joined ranks with the fourteen scouts sent up from Maryland. Captain Barrett was the leader of this group of frontiersmen who looked like they knew a thing or two about the woods. Most of the men were bearded and wore clothes like Gus or perhaps deer skin outfits. Captain Barrett would be the leader over all of the scouts. After watching him interact with the men, Gus decided that he liked the Captain because he seemed confident.

Gus noticed that some of the army Colonel Bouquet brought with him was made up of Highlanders from Scotland who wore red coats and blue plaid kilts. He had never seen a man in a kilt before and he found himself staring at them for some time. They also spoke with a funny accent. Gus had to listen hard to understand what the men were saying. They called each other "lads". There were also plenty of other German speaking men like himself from Pennsylvania who made up a large part of the army. The men from the Virginia militia who had come to join in were all English speaking, but they did not sound the same as the Scottish. It was indeed a strange mixture of people who were arranged in like speaking, sounding and looking groups as they prepared to make their way to Fort Pitt.

CHAPTER THIRTEEN

And so it was that with the scouts leading the way, Colonel Bouquet and his army left Fort Bedford and headed west on July 25th. Carl and John Watkins were issued muskets and supplies and marched along with the 60th Regiment of Foot. They were intent on getting back to save Fort Pitt. The army proceeded from the fort in columns of two men on each side of the supply wagons and pack horses. Members of Brigades 1,2,3,7,8 and 9 were on the right side and those of Brigades 4,5,6,10,11 and 12 were on the left. The cattle and sheep were at the rear under the watchful eyes of thirty men. Each unit had been prepared and knew what to do if they were attacked.

For the next few days, Gus got to know some of the men from Cumberland who made up half of the scouting party. As they walked along, they told stories about previous battles in western Pennsylvania. One of the first men to tell a story was man named Sergeant Caldwell. The scouts normally did not have a particular rank; Sergeant Caldwell had served in the Virginia militia and had achieved that rank. Even though he was now with the men in Maryland, he still referred to himself by his former title and the other scouts did as well. Gus kind of liked the Sergeant. He reminded him of his father, but he was not as old. As a result Gus found himself walking next to the Sergeant most of the time.

The first night of the march, after the men had eaten, Sergeant Caldwell said to Gus, "Young fella, do you know about how all this fightin' got started?"

"No, sir, I don't, but I know the Indians do not want us whites living in their homeland." replied Gus.

"Yes, that's true and we have a long history of fighting them and the French for the land we're headed for right now. I know a little about this mess because I've been in nearly every battle that's been fought for the past eleven years. It all began back in '53 when George Washington volunteered to take some fellow Virginia militia up to Fort LeBoeuf. They delivered a letter from the Lieutenant Governor telling the French to leave the Ohio Valley. Can you imagine what the response was? Young Mr. Washington was sent back to Virginia in a hurry. But on the way back, in his canoe he saw how important the fork where the two rivers meet to make the Ohio would be for a fort. He reported this to Lieutenant Governor Dinwiddie and the next year, Captain William Trent and one hundred men were sent back to build that fort. They worked hard to get the fort built, but were running out of supplies. Captain Trent went back to Maryland to get what was needed; leaving a fella named Ensign Edward Ward in charge. Well, he had just hung the gate on what he had called Fort Prince George when at least 500 French troops with cannons and many Indians appeared. Ward realized that he was badly outnumbered and simply left the fort to the French who moved right in, made some improvements on it and called it Fort Duquesne."

"There was no fighting?" protested Gus. "The men just walked away?"

"Yes, that is true, but that's how it began. Both the French and the British wanted the land over there. It is full of game and the waterways run all the way to the Gulf. Whoever controls that Ohio River valley controls trade, and trade is money."

"Oh," said Gus, "so it isn't just about the Indians?"

"No, I'm afraid that is only part of the issue. In fact the Indian problem we are now having was not the issue at all in the beginning."

After his talk with Sergeant Caldwell, Gus unrolled his blanket and lay down. The sky was clear and as he watched the stars, he wondered more about the conflict with the Indians. He hoped he would get a chance to ask Sergeant Caldwell some questions. He began to list them in his mind and as he was doing so, drifted off to sleep. He had finished his first day as an army scout. He was tired but not afraid. Surrounded by people like Sergeant Caldwell who seemed to know something about fighting Indians, gave Gus comfort. He would simply learn from them.

The next morning, Gus was awakened to the noise of men gathering together their gear and supplies. He quickly made a biscuit and warmed a piece of smoked ham. He did not like coffee and his family never drank rum, so he drank water from his tin canteen. Soon after he finished cleaning up, the order was given for the men to move out to continue the march to Fort Pitt.

The men walked for two hours at a time and rested for a bit in between. After each brief stop, the Colonel would give the order to move on. He was hoping to make seventeen miles a day, but the flour wagons were heavy and the going was not easy for the horses trying to pull them along. Gus did not have any trouble keeping up with the others. He was watching them to try to figure out just what he was supposed to be doing as a scout. One of the first things he noticed was that the men seldom looked straight ahead or down at the road. They were constantly looking off to the right or left, looking for movement that might indicate that Indians were watching. So Gus learned as he marched along.

That night they made it to Shawnee Cabins where they rested. As the men were gathered around a small fire, Sergeant Caldwell told a second story about all that had preceded their current march to Fort Pitt. "Now, this account is also one about George Washington and Governor Dinwiddie and a regiment of Virginia frontiersmen. I was one of them. It seems that after Washington had seen the forks of the Ohio, the Governor was determined to have himself a fort there. So, he sent Lieutenant Washington westward from Alexandria, Virginia, located right there on the Potomac River. He had under his command, a part of a regiment of Virginia frontiersmen who were to build a road to Redstone Creek over on the Monongahela River that leads up to the fork that makes the Ohio. From there we were supposed to make our way to the fort that Ensign Ward was building. It was hard work for all of us as we cut trees and pulled stumps. So, Lieutenant Washington had us working in shifts. When we weren't cutting, we were scouting the area to make sure no Indians were lurking about. Some of us were also assigned the responsibility of finding game to eat. There was plenty of that to be sure. We were able to find elk, deer, bear, raccoon and turkey without trying too hard."

After a brief pause, Caldwell continued, "Now, Colonel Joshua Fry, who was in command of the whole expedition, met Washington and the rest of us at Wills Creek with the rest of the Virginia Regiment, but unfortunately he died shortly after that. It was a shame. He seemed like a nice fella, and I never did know what was wrong with him.

"One day when I was out with some others hunting game, we came across a party of Indians. We didn't know what to do for sure. They didn't seem afraid of us and they didn't try to run off. It was a good thing that one of the men in our party realized they were Seneca Indians and knew enough of their language to talk to them some. They told us that the French had taken Fort Prince George.

"Well, as soon as we reported this new information to Lieutenant Washington, he decided that we could not take the fort with just one regiment, even though we were a pretty tough bunch. So, we proceeded to find a location about fifty miles away from the forks where he could build a fort and protect ourselves as we continued to build the road we were sent to build. Lieutenant Washington decided to build his fort at Great Meadows. It was a big open place that was not much more than a marsh."

"The fort we built was made of logs and fashioned in a circle. Washington called it his 'Fort of Necessity' because it was just that. Some folks called it Great Meadows, but those of us who were there called it a necessity. It wasn't much to look at, just logs stuck in the ground standing straight up like fence posts all side by side. But we thought it would offer us some protection from an attack.

"After the fort was built, we learned that a group of French soldiers had been spotted about seven miles away," Sergeant Caldwell said. "Lieutenant Washington and forty of us went out to find them. We reached the village of the friendly Seneca Indians who took us to a ravine about two miles away where the French were camped. On May 28th, of '54, we surprised this small French force, killing envoy Ensign Coulon de Jumonville, and ten of his soldiers. Another man was wounded and twenty one men were taken prisoner. Now, Gus, there was the first fighting. Men were killed by us and the Indians and it has not stopped since."

Everyone sat silently, taking in what Sergeant Caldwell had said. Many people had been killed during this time of war and unrest. Gus' parents were two of them.

Finally, Caldwell said, "I believe there were nearly three hundred of us at Fort Necessity, and then another hundred British fellas from Carolina came to help us. We kept on building a road all the way up to Gist's Plantation but then heard that the French were on their way to our position and we retreated to Fort Necessity. They must have had Indian spies or maybe they missed them soldiers we killed. Someone suggested that one of them may have snuck away after our attack. I can't say for sure.

"It was in early June of '54 that the French and their Indian friends attacked us at Fort Necessity. There must have been 700 of them shooting at us from behind every rise, tree, bush and rock. They were all around us and it seemed like the firing was constant.

"After a full day of fighting, and with a third of his officers either wounded or killed, Lieutenant Washington was forced to surrender his command. The French commander was Captain Louis Colon de Villiers. I found out that he was the brother of the Ensign Jumonville who we had killed earlier in that ravine.

"I was surprised that the French let us retreat back to Maryland and Virginia. Maybe Captain de Villiers figured we had reinforcements coming or something, but all of us that had survived the battle were free to go. And that is just what we did as fast as we could. Yes sir, Lieutenant Washington did not have to tell us twice to pack up and march out. We were just happy to be alive! Those Indians made the darnedest sounds, shouting, hooting and scaring us all half to death."

Having heard these accounts of the war, Gus was concerned that fighting these Indians was not going to be easy. After each story, Gus asked himself why he had signed up. None of the previous leaders were able to defeat the Indians who knew the forest and how to fight from behind trees rather than out in the open wearing bright red coats and red hats with black fur. He could hear Elizabeth telling him not to get killed. When he closed his eyes that night, he began to think that he might not make it back to the one he loved. He lay on the ground and covered up even though it was not too cold. He knew that his blanket would not protect him. He kept it on anyway.

CHAPTER FOURTEEN

The next morning, the soldiers lined up again as they had when they marched out of Fort Bedford. By now they were walking up hill and when the wagons got stuck, they were told to push from behind to give the horses some relief. After walking about half a day, the men were allowed to stop for a rest and a chance to eat something. Many of the frontiersmen had jerky they ate and some water to drink from their canteen. The second half of the day was much the same as the first, only the hills were steeper. Gus and the scouts did not have to push the wagons but were asked to carry some extra supplies that belonged to the men who were pushing. By evening, they had nearly made it half way up the Blue Mountains and knew that the next day would be just as rough going as the day they had just spent. The men were all exhausted and looked forward to some rest.

While relaxing around the cook fire that night, Sergeant Caldwell and some others began to talk about another battle that Gus had heard something about when he was younger. This one also involved Lieutenant Washington from Virginia, but now he was a Colonel. The British force he was with was led by a man named Braddock. Sergeant Caldwell said, "The year after Washington was defeated at Fort Necessity, the British decided to send a force of nearly fifteen hundred men under the leadership of Major General Edward Braddock to expel the French from Fort Duquesne. General Braddock was determined to take the fort and so he brought with him huge siege cannons. Washington had volunteered to be Braddock's aide as the army made its way to Fort Duquesne and Daniel Boone was also with us. But this Englishman was an arrogant fella. I heard a story about a time when he and Dr. Franklin from here in Pennsylvania were having dinner and discussing this expedition. According to the story, Dr. Franklin tried to warn him that fighting the Indians would not be easy, but he replied, 'The Indians may be formidable to your raw American militia; upon the king's regulars and disciplined troops, it is impossible they should make an impression.' Can you believe that?

"Well, he felt that the Indian guides who were going to help us were of little or no value. They knew it and many just up and left us along the way. One of the chiefs, Minacatootha, from the Oneida tribe, reported to Mr. Franklin that Braddock looked upon the Indians as if they were dogs and would never listen to anything they told him.

"I was with Washington again. We began our trip from Fort Cumberland along Wills Creek the first week of June, as I recall. But, General Braddock had about 500 pioneers go ahead of us to clear the pathway and collect stores at Fort Necessity. We even had fifty sailors who had experience with rigging of all sorts. They came in handy as we tried to get all of our supplies over the mountains. He then relegated the militia to chopping trees and driving supply wagons. When he was ready, Braddock marched his 2,200 man army into the wilderness hacking out a road towards Fort Duquesne. The French easily followed Braddock's slow progress, but without help from the Delaware, Shawnee, and Mingo, they found it difficult to supply their forts. Since not one Delaware and only four Shawnee warriors were willing to help them to defend Fort Duquesne, they were forced to bring 300 French and 600 Indian allies from Canada and the Great Lakes.

"Well, I'll tell you, we moved along slower than a turtle. In the first ten days, we only made twenty-six miles! Washington persuaded General Braddock to allow him and Sir Peter Halket to move out with a part of the army in light marching order, along with the artillery. By leaving the rest of the baggage train behind, the army could advance more quickly and hopefully get to Fort Duquesne before the French could reinforce it. We forged ahead with this force of fourteen hundred men and artillery. Our confidence was strong as we began that hundred and thirty mile march. Encouraged by our numbers and the confidence of our leadership, we pressed on. With the militia out front we had made our way to within about ten miles of the fort and everyone was being careful. Fortunately we had no problems to that point. The main force had caught up to us and we began to make our final move for we were less than a day's march away from the fort. We thought that the French may try to come out and attack us along the way, especially as we tried to ford the Monongahela River at Turtle Creek. We were all quite relieved when we made this crossing unmolested. The scouts had found shallow areas for us to cross and the officers kept reminding us to keep our powder dry. I think we all knew better than to go for a swim, but they seemed to like to give instruction. We had expected to be attacked in several places, but now it seemed that maybe the French were going to wait to engage us at their fort.

"I was not an officer or anything," continued Caldwell, "but I happened to hear Colonel Washington and General Braddock discussing how to proceed from where we were. The general had the troops all lined up in solid platoons, but Washington encouraged him to send us out in open order and to use the Indian or frontier style of fighting if we were attacked in the forest between our present position and the fort. Well, I'll tell you, Major General Braddock was mad. He said, 'What! A provisional Colonel teach a British general how to fight!' And that ended that conversation. We marched out in solid platoons.

"Just after noon, on July 9th, about a month into our march, and just about ten miles from Fort Duquesne, Lieutenant Colonel Thomas Gage and his force of 300 men rounded a bend on a narrow road with a rise of land to the right. Some of us from the Virginia militia were with them at the time. All of a sudden the scouts came rushing back saying that they had just seen a large force of French and Indians coming their way. Gage ordered us to line up, and when the French approached, we opened fire, killing Captain Beaujeau, the French commander. The second in command took charge and the French Regulars stayed in front, forming a crescent shape, while the Indians who were with them began pouring down both our flanks under cover of the forest. Heavy musket fire and a steady stream of arrows began to tear into our ranks. Along with the bullets and arrows came the war whoops of the Indians that served to frighten the British regulars more than the gun fire. Colonel Gage attempted to withdraw, but lagging behind us was a work party that was still advancing. Those of us who were retreating ran smack dab into the advancing work party and that caused even more confusion.

"We couldn't see the Indians who continued to move around us in the trees but we could hear them. The best the British could do was form a square and fire blindly into the woods. We militia followed suit but seemed to fair little better. I know we fired quite a bit, but the Indians were all around us and we did not know for sure what to do except continue to fire into the woods at targets we could hardly see. In short order, the British officers were being targeted by the enemy. It seemed like many of the officers were killed or wounded. The Indians must have been told to kill the men on horseback first. Those under their command began to panic once their officer was killed. The rest of the officers tried to rally the troops, to bring about order, but the war whoops of the Indians and the death all around us frightened even those of us who had fought these Indians before."

"That must have been terrifying," said one of the men from Cumberland.

"It was," replied Sergeant Caldwell, "and to make matters worse, the baggage train that followed behind ran right into the back of the work party making any escape impossible and delaying any reinforcements from the main party. Washington told us later that when Major General Braddock heard the gunfire, he led the bulk of his troops forward to join the fighting. Now, for the second time those of us in the front being fired upon from three sides, could not escape. Our own army was pouring in just as we were trying to get out. We were surrounded by the French and their Indians and bottled up by our own army. When Braddock finally made it to the fighting, I saw his horse get shot right out from under him. In fact, others told me he had four horses shot out from under him before it was all over. He tried repeatedly to rally the troops, but men were trying to get away and standing there firing at trees did not seem to make a lot of sense. Colonel Washington rode forward at one point and pleaded with Braddock to allow him to scatter 300 of us militia throughout the trees to fight Indian fashion, but was once again rebuked. This time I thought he was going to run Washington through with his saber for he drew it up and replied, 'I've a mind to run you through the body. We'll sup today in Fort Duquesne or else die in hell!' He should have listened to Washington. It was a slaughter for the British Regulars. At one point, the French captured two cannon from the British regulars and turned the guns on us."

"What happened next?" asked Gus. "How did you survive?"

"Well, when the cannon started firing at us, we men from Virginia scattered and soon began to fight back just like the Indians. We were doing a little better, but then some of the British regulars thought we were Indians and started firing at us, too. General Braddock decided to try to get the high ground on the right so that we might have some advantage, but the attempt failed. He was wounded and without his leadership, it seemed the troops just gave up. On top of that, the British regulars had fired so often at nothing that many of them had used up all of the twenty-four rounds they had been issued when we left on this expedition. They tried to retreat and were cut down from all sides. After that, Washington decided to retreat and save whatever lives and supplies he could. I guess I was one of the lucky ones. The battle had lasted about two hours. Of the eighty-six English officers, sixty-three were killed or wounded, including Sir Peter Halket. Of Braddock's staff, only George Washington was alive and relatively well. In addition, one half of the private soldiers were killed or wounded. And we left behind artillery, guns, ammunition, and wagons full of supplies, horses, cattle, and gold.

"We did get Major General Braddock out of the fighting. But he was badly wounded and died from his wounds a few days later. His last words were reported to me to be 'Who would have thought it?' General Washington had us bury him in the center of the road he had just built so that the Indians would not find his body and desecrate it. Those of us who were left headed for Fort Necessity.

"On the way back to Virginia, I heard General Washington recount that he had one horse killed, and two wounded under him, a ball through his hat, and several through his clothes, but, he had escaped unhurt. He too was lucky, for with us on our night retreat were many wounded, some of whom simply could not keep up and were left to die along the road."

"But we took care of some of those Indians," a man from Pennsylvania chimed in. "The reaction of most of us to the news of Braddock's defeat was stunned disbelief followed by rage. Some of the officials from Pennsylvania seized and hanged a Delaware-Shawnee delegation sent to protest the Iroquois sale of Ohio."

"Yes, but that action seemed to make things worse," commented a member of the Virginia militia. "The neutrality of the Delaware and Shawnee ended with an outpouring of rage. Their attacks on the Pennsylvania, Maryland and Virginia frontiers were never intended to support the French but to punish the British. By 1758, I heard that more than 2,500 colonists had been killed—the greatest loss suffered by the British in this conflict and an explanation for the hatreds harbored by the "Long Knives", the name the Indians gave to the Pennsylvania and Virginia frontiersmen, when they began to occupy the Ohio Valley. Shingas, now known as "Shingas the Terrible", raided settlements along the Susquehanna and invited the Delaware living there under Iroquois supervision to join his war parties. At first they refused, but the raids created such hatred among the colonists, the eastern Delaware went over the edge."

After the stories were over, the men each found their own bed rolls and soon there was no more conversation but only silence. The stories and the images in his head began to concern Gus. He found it difficult to sleep and listened intently to the forest sounds all around him. He began to worry about what he had gotten himself into. So far, all he had heard from the older men were stories about losses and people dying. This fighting was not going to be easy. And he certainly did not want to be one who died. Elizabeth would kill him!

CHAPTER FIFTEEN

After breakfast, Colonel Bouquet cautioned Captain Barrett to make sure the scouts were attentive for the march ahead. The army was only a few days from Fort Ligonier, but it was also a few days away from Fort Bedford. Bouquet thought that the dense woods along the road would be an ideal place for an attack. The army would be spread out and tired out from pushing, pulling and marching. He promised to take a few more rests during this march as they crested the mountains, but he wanted the scouts to be attentive and to walk well out in front and to the sides of the main party. And so they departed. Gus was using all his skills and all his senses to try to pick up any sign of Indians in the area. The others scouts around him were doing the same as they checked out potential hiding places and peered deeply into the woods.

After a few hours, one of the scouts called to Captain Barrett and when he arrived, he showed him the remains of a camp fire and bones that had been burned. Someone had had a meal at this site just the day before. The ground was too dry to see foot prints, but it was clear that several people had slept under the tree near the fire.

This news made everyone pay special attention. They all knew they were being watched, but this was the first proof they had found. Now they knew they had to be careful.

The cautiousness of the scouts slowed the pace of the march. Gus looked more closely into the dense underbrush and listened for any signs of people moving through the woods. Though he did not hear anything, he did notice the dark green leaves of a mountain laurel moving when there was not apparent breeze.

The movement made him stop and focus in the bush. He held up his hand and signaled to the man closest to him to quietly make his way around behind the bush. As he stood there with his musket pointed at the bush, out from behind waddled a skunk. Gus and the other scout ran off in opposite directions hoping the skunk would not be frightened and spray them. Some of the other scouts saw them running and they stopped to see what was going on. When they saw the skunk, the other men started chuckling and soon the chuckles turned into a laughter and then into teasing about being afraid of a poor little polecat. Gus took it all in good fun, and the episode broke up the tension in the air among the scouts.

They finally got back to scouting and the march continued. The day ended much like the one before. The men were tired after a long day of marching and assisting the wagons up and down the hills. When they camped that night, they were high in the mountains and headed toward Fort Ligonier. As they settled in around cooking fires, one of the men from the Pennsylvania militia began to tell a story about a missionary he admired named Christian Fredrick Post. He was a Moravian who had worked among the Indians in Pennsylvania and had some success in befriending them and earning their trust.

"Well," said the militiaman, "Rev. Post had been working with the Indians in Western Pennsylvania and Ohio for some time. He was not seen as a threat to the Indians, so they left him alone. He traveled from one village to another talking to the chiefs and the spiritual leaders. Over time, some Indians actually began to follow his teachings about God."

"I never knew there were Christian Indians," said Gus.

"Oh yes," replied the militiaman. "And when the word spread of Rev. Post's achievements, General Forbes sent for him and persuaded him to convince the Delaware and other warring tribes to abandon their support of the French and make peace with the British. So, Rev. Post began his mission by traveling deep into the

Ohio Country with a small entourage of Indian guides to counsel with the notable Delaware chief, Tamaqua, and others such as King Beaver.

"At this time, General Forbes was making plans to move westward from Philadelphia to attack the French at Fort Duquesne. The general, eager to avoid what had happened to Braddock three years before, hoped that Post could persuade the Indians to deny aid to the French. In return, Forbes pledged that, once the French were driven off and defeated, the British would also retire back across the mountains, making the area a permanent Indian sanctuary.

"As Rev. Post made his way across the Pennsylvania frontier, he could not help but notice the devastation wrought by three years of war. I remember the preacher of my church reading us a letter from him one Sunday. In it he said something like 'It gave me great pain, to observe many farms deserted and laid waste; and I could not but reflect on the distress, the poor owners must be drove to, who once lived in plenty.'

"The poor missionary must have realized that his task to convince the Indians to make peace would not be easy. Along the way, Rev. Post reported to us that one of the Indian guides asked him, 'Why do not you and the French fight on the sea? You come here only to cheat the poor Indians, and take their land from them.'

"After a long and tiring journey, visiting many villages, Rev. Post finally arrived at Kuskuski, an important Delaware village located along the Shenango River. While there conferring with Chief Tamaqua and other Native leaders, Rev. Post had an opportunity to survey the village and learn something of Indian customs. He reported that many of the things we think about Indians are not true. Far from being savages, they are deeply spiritual and engage in many rituals designed to invoke blessings from the 'Master of Life,' the term they use for God. All they wish for is to be secure in their homeland and raise their children in peace."

"If that is so, why did they kill my parents and take their scalps?" asked Gus.

The militia man thought for a moment and said, "Why do we kill? Are we any better?"

No one seemed to have an answer to either question, so the militia man continued, "During Post's negotiations with the Indian chiefs, he learned that they were greatly concerned over the large British army that they heard was being formed to come to Fort Duquesne. One leader told the missionary, 'We have great reason to believe you intend to drive us away, and move into the country; or else why do you come to fight in the land that God has given us?' Post assured Tamaqua and the others of the sincerity of his message. To prove this, the Indians asked Post to return to the east and bring back 'the great belt of peace,' a sacred strap made from leather and decorated with shell beads known as wampum."

"Post kept his promise and returned to the Indian villages in the Ohio Country in October, just as General Forbes prepared for his final push toward Fort Duquesne. The Indians accepted the peace belt and moved their villages away from the French fort."

Gus knew that there were some missionaries who worked with the Indians, but had never heard of Rev. Post. He wondered why Rev. McGregor was not like him in his attitude toward plain folk. If Gus was not good enough, he could never imagine Rev. McGregor ever living with Indians. That thought made him smile. No, he would never do that.

CHAPTER SIXTEEN

The next morning, the men got up and ate a quick breakfast of biscuits and gravy. Some of them had jerky and chewed on it as they drank their coffee. Afterwards they cleaned up, packed up and prepared to continue their march westward. Gus had been carrying his tomahawk in his belt during the trip thus far and had not really tried to throw it like some of the men were able to. He decided to practice taking the tomahawk out and tossing it into a tree trunk fifteen feet away. It bounced off the tree many more times than it stuck, but when it did stick, Gus celebrated. He decided that he should not expect to use the tomahawk unless his life was in danger and he had no gun or knife. He would continue to practice each day because one never knew when that situation might occur.

Gus and the other scouts were in the lead once again. As they walked along, the men tried to look and listen for signs that might alert them to any Indians that might be waiting for them. They did not see anything too unusual as they made their way along but kept up their intensity because they knew that the lives of many soldiers and pioneers depended on their talents. Fortunately, all of these scouts could track and read signs unlike the men from the 44th Regiment who had gotten lost as they marched from Carlisle.

After about ten miles of walking, the army stopped for a lunch break. They had not seen any Indians during the first half of the day. As they ate, Gus found himself listening to the stories of Sergeant Caldwell. But finally, this story was one that had good news. It was the story about General John Forbes. Gus knew a little of this story because a part of it involved Fort Bedford, but he did not want to prevent Sergeant Caldwell from telling it all the way through. Caldwell began by pointing out that once again the Virginia militia worked hand-in-hand with the British regulars in this attempt to capture Fort Duquesne.

"Let me think. I believe it was in the summer of '58 when General Forbes was ready to try once again to take Fort Duquesne from the French. Some of us wondered what he was going to do that General Braddock was unable to do before him, but we were encouraged when Lt. Colonel Washington once again was selected to serve as the aide to the General. And, you might be interested to know that he also had a Swiss-born Colonel of the Royal American Regiment serving under him, a man some of you may know as our own Colonel Henry Bouquet."

"Then he knows this road we travel?" asked one of the men.

"Yes, he does, in more ways than one. You see, he helped build it. General Forbes' plan was to complete a slow and methodical march to Fort Duquesne. He took great pains to secure his lines of supply and communication with a string of forts that led from Philadelphia to Fort Duquesne. Fort Carlisle, Fort Littleton, Fort Bedford and the one we are going to on the other side of this mountain range are all a part of his plan. Colonel Bouquet was the one that he sent ahead to build this string of forts. While the engineers were building the forts, Colonel Bouquet was drilling his troops to fight a new kind of war. He had been with Braddock and had seen how the Indians fought. He decided to use scouts like us to walk in silence and investigate any areas where a group of Indians may be hiding in wait. General Forbes said that he wanted to build a new road to Fort Duquesne so as not to cross so many rivers as Braddock had when he came across the mountains from Cumberland. This also gave the tactical advantage of forcing the French to divide their assets and defend both approaches. That Forbes was a smart man. We could see that he had planned ahead and that put us at ease.

"We had plenty of men this time around, too," continued Sergeant Caldwell. "There were nearly 7,000 regular and provincial troops and we made one heck of a big army. We had the 60th Royal American Regiment and a detachment of the 77th Regiment of Foot along with colonial troops from Pennsylvania, Virginia, Delaware, Maryland and North Carolina. General Forbes had us cutting our way right across Pennsylvania. The road was wide enough for the wagons we brought. We didn't care if the noise attracted attention, there were so many of us that we were sure we scared the Indians who were watching our progress."

"As we were nearing the fort, General Forbes sent Major James Grant of Ballindalloch, who was the commander of the 77th Regiment of Foot, the same regiment that is marching with us this very day, out ahead on a night mission." Caldwell paused a minute then said, "I wasn't there, mind you, but the accounts go that Major Grant was supposed to be on this night mission to check out Fort Duquesne ahead of the rest of us and destroy any Indian camps in the area. After that he was supposed to withdraw to try to get the Indians to follow him. Then he was supposed to have his men line up on both sides of the trail and ambush those who followed. He had about 350 men all together. For some reason, he did not do what he was told. He set fire to some out buildings, and remained on a hillside outside the fort to watch. He must have thought that the French were too weak to attack him, so he sent one hundred Highlanders down the hill, straight toward the fort. Well, he was wrong. The French and their Indian allies numbered around eight hundred and they came out and quickly encircled these Scottish soldiers. Grant and the rest of his army then tried to rescue the first one hundred and soon found themselves also hemmed in on all sides. The Indians were firing from the trees just like they did with Braddock. Hearing firing coming from the direction of the fort, the troops Grant held in ambush along the trail also rushed forward and joined the fight. Confusion reigned as the Major attempted to rally his troops, but eventually the men broke off and retreated. I'm told that the Scotts fought bravely but inflicted little damage to the French who had come out to meet them. The story I was told was that 100 of the Pennsylvanians deserted without firing a shot. The Virginians fought on until forced to retreat. Major Grant was then taken prisoner as were about twenty of his men. But the poor Scotts lost over two hundred men."

Gus wondered as he heard the account of the men from Pennsylvania running away what he would have done. He was a bit ashamed of these men and at the same time wondered what he might do when the time came that he was under fire. He knew it would. A part of him wanted it to happen soon and another part hoped that he would never have to know for sure what he would do if surrounded by the enemy. In the end he decided that he would kill as many as he could. He had promised himself that. Then maybe he would desert. The idea made him smile. He honestly did not know what he would do. Time would tell.

"With this defeat," continued Sergeant Caldwell, "General Forbes decided to settle down for the winter at Fort Ligonier and wait until the spring to attack. But, a few days later, we were attacked by the French at the fort that was not quiet finished yet. I suppose they figured that they should strike while the iron was hot. The battle lasted four hours and the French were beaten back, though they did take most of the horses. Only about twelve of our men were killed, eighteen were wounded and a few were missing. I assume they were killed or taken captive. During the attack, we captured a few prisoners. One of them was a young man named Johnson. That didn't sound a like a French name to me. Come to find out he had been captured many years earlier by the Indians in Lancaster. When the general talked to him, he found out that the French had less than five hundred troops in the fort and that the Indians had all moved away.

"The General learned after his little chat with Mr. Johnson that Conrad Weiser arbitrated a council at Easton, Pennsylvania, near Philadelphia, during which the tribes in the Ohio Valley agreed to abandon the French. This collapse of Indian support was a major factor in General Forbes' next decision. After the information was confirmed, the General decided to launch an immediate attack on the weakened fort. He divided us up into three columns in preparation to make the final assault on the fortress. But the French, who were now hopelessly outnumbered, abandoned and razed Fort Duquesne before we could get there.

"We occupied the burned fort on November 25th of '58 without firing a shot. But the sight we saw as we marched to the point of the rivers, I'll never forget. When we marched up to the smoldering remains, I'll tell you, I nearly cried. The Indians had cut off the heads of many of the dead Highlanders and impaled them on the sharp wooden stakes on top of the fort walls. And below their heads were hung their green and blue plaid kilts. I recognized some of these men. Captain Mackenzie, Lieutenant MacDonald and Ensign Grant were the ones I knew whose heads were up on the posts. General Forbes immediately had a detail remove the heads and kilts and bury the rotting remains that were found around the Fort where they were killed.

John and Carl Watkins had been listening to this story and they finally chimed in.

John said, "One of the Colonels from the Pennsylvania militia, by the name of John Armstrong, personally planted their flag over Fort Duquesne. He was the same man who led the group of rangers to Kittanning to rescue the McCord women who had been taken when their husbands and sons were killed at Fort McCord in '56. These were the same Indians who had killed his brother. He got his revenge."

"Yes," Carl said, "for many months, two Indian leaders, Captain Jacobs and Shingas the Terrible, used this village as a staging area to launch raids against our defenseless frontier folks. The forts Mr. Franklin had built did not stop all of the attacks. The Indians snuck by the defensive line of forts to resume their horrific raiding activities against the hapless settlers living in the Great Cove, at Sherman's Valley, and along the Conococheague. Emboldened by their raiding success, Shingas and Captain Jacobs led their Delaware warriors in attacks against the smaller stockades, beginning this past spring. Patterson's Fort was attacked. The following day, the Indians succeeded in capturing McCord's Fort, killing or capturing a total of 27 persons.

"These attacks reached their high point around the end of July when Fort Granville fell to the Delaware. In this strike, the Indians were able to creep close enough to the wooden palisade to shoot fire arrows into the wall. Unable to defend the fort, the garrison surrendered. In all, 23 soldiers, along with a number of women and children, were killed or taken back to Kittanning as captives. One of the dead soldiers was Lieutenant Edward Armstrong, brother of Colonel John Armstrong of the Pennsylvania militia.

"Vowing revenge, Colonel Armstrong proposed to Governor Robert Morris that one battalion of the Pennsylvania Regiment march to Kittanning to destroy the Indian stronghold. As a result, the Colonel, with about 300 men, set out from Fort Shirley near the end of August. By the fourth day of September, the command had advanced to within 50 miles of the Indian village. From this point, Colonel Armstrong sent scouts to locate and spy on the Indian camp. When these men returned, they reported the Indians were indeed in the village. After resuming his march, Colonel Armstrong and his men reached a hill overlooking the river and village that was located on its banks on the evening of September 7th. At dawn the soldiers prepared for battle by creeping silently down the hill, towards the sleeping Indian village.

"According to Colonel Armstrong's report, when the first shots were fired, Captain Jacobs immediately gave the war whoop, and cried, 'The white men have at last come. We will soon have scalps enough.' The troops quickly surrounded the encampment and set fire to a number of Indian cabins. The Indians inside these cabins ran out to escape the flames but were quickly shot down by the Pennsylvanians. At one point during the raid, Colonel Armstrong noted that 'Captain Jacobs tumbled himself out a loft window, and was shot.' Several captives freed during the attack identified the Delaware leader's body. In the end, Captain Jacobs and perhaps as many as 30 Indians were killed in the raid, and Colonel Armstrong and his men recovered seven captives being held by the Indians. Believing he had inflicted enough damage and fearful the Indians would soon be reinforced by the French from Fort Duquesne, Colonel Armstrong ordered a retreat from the smoldering village.

"Now, the way I see it, Armstrong's victory marked the first time, since the defeat of Colonel Washington at Fort Necessity, that British subjects have been able to vanquish the enemy in battle. And mind you, they was all Pennsylvanians doing the fighting that time."

"Yes, that is the case," replied Sergeant Caldwell, "but you have to admit, the Pennsylvania militia was not as involved as we men from Virginia from the beginning. We did most of the fighting right along."

"That's true," replied Carl, "and most of the loosing!"

That got a laugh from the men, but it was all meant in fun. They were on the same side now and could tease a little.

Finally, Sergeant Caldwell continued, "When the flag had been raised at the smoldering remains of Fort Duquesne, and the bodies properly buried, General Forbes ordered the construction of a new fortification to be named Fort Pitt, after British Secretary of State William Pitt. He also named the settlement between the rivers "Pittsborough". It is this fort, gentlemen, that is under siege. I'll be happy to see her again and just as happy when I leave. It seems like there is always a problem when I make my way toward that spot where the Ohio River begins.

The temperature in the winter, at the point, fell to a bone-chilling 14 degrees and it was impossible to sustain such a large army at Fort Pitt. Therefore, General Forbes, who was desperately ill, decided to withdraw back to Philadelphia, leaving behind a small force under Colonel Hugh Mercer to hold this strategic region until spring. The plan was for the army to return to drive the French from their forts to the north. Before General Forbes departed, Rev. Post and a delegation of Indians came to Fort Pitt to confer with him. The Indians came to obtain assurances from the British that they would depart from the region and leave the land to the west of the Allegheny Mountains as a permanent Indian homeland."

Other soldiers talked about other battles or skirmishes they had fought in or heard about. They talked about Pontiac and what they had heard about his attempt to take Fort Detroit. The story was told by an older man whose name Gus did not know. He said, "Pontiac offered to come to the fort to perform a ceremonial dance for the British. But what they really wanted to do was size up the opposition. He told the post commander, a man named Major Gladwin, that he would like to come back again a few days later for a good-will council. His real plan, you see, was to have all his warriors come back into the fort carrying concealed knives, tomahawks and sawed off muskets under their blankets. Somehow Major Gladwin learned of the plan and when Pontiac returned with his warriors, he was not permitted access. Furious, Pontiac ordered his warriors to kill any Englishmen they could find, but to spare the French. From that moment on, the Fort at Detroit has been under siege. It's the only one besides Fort Pitt that still remains in our control in all the Ohio valley."

The man continued by telling his story. He said, "A man named Captain James Dalyell with 260 men, including some of Roger's Rangers, was sent to help the 130 soldiers at Fort Detroit. They were successful at reaching the fort, but when they attempted to search for Pontiac, they were ambushed as they crossed a narrow bridge over a creek. Captain Dalyell led a charge into the Ottawa position and was killed along with nearly twenty other men. In addition, nearly thirty-five were wounded and many more were captured. The creek ran red with the blood of the English soldiers and the battle was christened the battle of Bloody Run."

The story made Gus wonder if he and his new friends were walking into an ambush as well. He would have to be very attentive and use all of his skills to help his friends and the people at Fort Pitt.

CHAPTER SEVENTEEN

When Captain Ecuyer reported to the chiefs surrounding Fort Pitt, that there was an army coming, the Delaware chiefs decided to meet with the chiefs of the other tribes to determine what they should do. Some did not believe Captain Ecuyer and wanted to attack the fort. Others wanted to simply wait like they had planned. But in the end, the best idea came from one of the Mingo chiefs. He suggested that they wait where they were, but that they send out scouts who could see an army coming and then quickly return to the fort to let them know the details.

The Indians sent out several warriors from each tribe. Some were sent to Forbes Road that ran east from Fort Pitt to Fort Ligonier. Some were sent to the road Washington was building that came up from Virginia and followed the Monongahela River. Some were sent to watch along the rivers coming up from Virginia and down from the great lakes. These warriors were sent in pairs, so that if they saw anything, one would return right away with the news and size of the army while the other watched to see where it was going. If it was making its way to Fort Pitt, he would do the same and try to give as much information as possible about the approaching enemy.

Each chief selected his own warriors and sent them on their way with the appropriate instructions. Chief Natawatwees selected his oldest son, Tamany, and was about to select another warrior when Newate stood before him and asked if he could go. He reasoned that he could be the one to return with the information since he was a fast runner. At first the chief was reluctant, but he finally agreed. There was a fear that his youngest son may get hurt, but after he thought about it, he decided that Newate would be hidden and not try to confront the soldiers in any way. This may give him some good experience, and besides, there was nothing to do at the camp site but wait. So he agreed and after giving the brothers and several other warriors that he had selected their final instructions, he sent them on their way.

The warrior scouts were all sent out, spread in every direction but west into their homeland. Some went up the Allegheny toward Kittanning where the Pennsylvania militia killed Captain Jacobs and other Indians. Others followed the road south east toward Virginia where Braddock was defeated and lost his life. Natawatwees sent his sons and the others east along the road made by Forbes that led to Fort Ligonier and from there, over the mountains to Fort Bedford.

Newate and Tamany began to make their journey eastward. They had some food with them, but stopped at the streams to catch fish and set some snares for rabbit. These items did not require the use of muskets, but skill, and both these Indians were very skilled at living off the land.

The brothers avoided the main road, but walked parallel to it so they could hear and see if anyone was marching along. As they walked, Newate asked his brother, "What does it feel like to be in battle?"

"It is both frightening and exciting. You do not think about what you should do, you simply respond. You act. And if you are lucky, you are quicker or stronger than the person who is trying to kill you."

"Do you think we will be able to win this battle with the white soldiers?" asked Newate.

"These men fight like women." was the reply.

"Like the one who gave you the scar?" teased Newate.

"If they are lucky, they may get that close. But I am not worried about them. We have a large army of our own. And we know how to fight in these woods. Those men stand there waiting to be shot."

"Are they brave?" asked Newate.

"No, they are not brave and they are not very smart. Who would stand out in the open and let us shoot them?" asked his brother.

"Well," said Newate, "I hope you're right. I do not have much hair up there, but I would like to keep it."

"Don't worry, most of the white men do not scalp; just the frontiersmen."

"Are they any better fighters than the regular soldiers?" Newate asked.

"Yes, they fight like we do from behind tree, rocks and bushes."

As the brothers found a place to stay the first night, they ate some of the dried deer meat they brought from home and drank water from a small stream. Then they found a pine tree and curled up underneath it on the soft bed of needles.

The next morning, Newate and his brother continued their travel westward. They found some berries and ate them as they made their way. By noon, both men were hungry and decided to look for some small game to kill. Newate found a ground hog hole and they decided that if they burned some dry leaves near the entrance the groundhog would pop out another hole to get away. So, they searched for other holes he might use as a exit and found two. Newate started a fire near the first hole and they each waited outside the other holes. It did not take long for the groundhog to come scurrying out the hole where Newate's brother was waiting. As soon as it appeared, he shot it with his bow and arrow. After it was skinned and cleaned, the brothers cooked it over a fire. They did not stay by the roasting groundhog, but hid in the forest nearby, in the event someone might smell the smoke and come to investigate. Their job was to be the ones who found the whites, not the ones to be found by the white men.

The lunch took longer than the brothers wanted. When the groundhog was cooked, they both ate until they could eat no more. Newate always ate like he had a hollow leg. His brother teased him about it, but Newate replied, "I'm still growing. If I keep eating like this, someday I'll be as big as you."

"You might get to be a big as me, but you will never be as handsome!"

They laughed and put out the fire and left the rest of the uneaten groundhog for the animals to finish.

The brothers continued to make their way eastward the rest of the day and were very attentive to any noises coming from the nearby road. There was nothing to raise their attention, so they walked on until nightfall. Then they ate some more of the dried meat and found another soft place to rest.

As the sun came up on the third day, Newate and Tamany decided to walk until they came across a stream where they might be able to catch a fish or something else to eat. They were such good shots that any large bird or small animal could be easily shot and cooked. Within an hour they came across a stream. The brothers watched carefully to see if there were fish swimming in it. They noticed many small ones but none big enough for a meal. A noise behind them, however, revealed what would do nicely. There in a tall oak tree sat a red tailed hawk squawking it's warning to all who would hear that it was nearby. Today, that warning brought about the attention of two hungry Indians and within seconds two arrows were flying in its direction. The bird jumped off its perch and avoided one arrow, but in doing so, flew into the path of the other.

Once again a small fire was made and the Indians plucked the feathers and cleaned the bird so they could cook it. Newate admired the long red tail feathers of the bird and decided that he would stick one of them into his head band so that it stuck up in the air in the back of his head.

Tamany warned him, "Be careful someone does not mistake you for a bird and shoot you. Not only would you be dead, but mom would kill me!"

They laughed as they hid in the nearby trees so they were between the roasting bird and the road. They took turns running out from the trees and turning the bird until it was cooked through. The fire was put out quickly and the brothers, again, took the food to another location that was partially hidden and enjoyed the meal.

By the end of that third day, Newate and his brother had come upon a settlement that had a British outpost. The older brother knew of this place and led Newate around it to avoid detection. After they had circled around the settlement, Tamany suggested that they walk a few more days until they neared Fort Ligonier. And so they walked on several more days, stopping to hunt and eat and sleep, while being as quiet as they could, anticipating the approaching army any day.

Five days after they left Fort Pitt, Newate and Tamany came upon a large stream and followed it to a small clearing where they could camp. They had no idea how long they would be there, so they used their tomahawks to cut some branches to make the roof of a lean-to. The front that was opened faced the east and the back that was enclosed faced the west, the direction from which the winds and rains normally came. The small shelter would help to keep them dry if they encountered a rainy day.

While his brother finished the lean-to, Newate went to the stream and made himself a spear to catch a fish or two for dinner. He used his usual method of standing right in the middle of the stream just a still as he could. Within a few minutes, he noticed a rainbow trout making its way along the bottom. Newate stabbed it with his spear and pulled it out of the water. He laid it on the bank and it flopped around for a few minutes until dying on its side in the tall grass. Encouraged by his success, Newate went back to the stream and stood waiting for another fish. After what seemed like a long time, another did swim by and Newate was able to stab it and take it to the banks of the stream. Just as he was getting out, his brother came over and they each cleaned a fish and cut off the head and tail. They cut two small cooking branches that were Y shaped and laid the fish on top of them so they could cook them over a fire.

Newate searched for firewood while his brother gathered some stones to make a fire circle and two larger Y shaped branches to place in the ground to support the ones the fish were now laying on.

After a short time the fish were done and the brothers enjoyed their first meal in their new outpost. As soon as the cooking was over, they put out the fire. Newate suggested that he go over by the road a watch for a few hours until it was dark and then in the morning they could begin taking turns watching the road. With this as an agreed upon plan, he was off and their watching and waiting began.

CHAPTER EIGHTEEN

Finally, Colonel Bouquet and his army crossed the Alleghenies and were coming down the western slopes that led to Fort Ligonier. As they crossed a stream of crystal clear water called the Loyalhanna, the men stopped to fill their canteens and rest. The water was cool and refreshing as it tumbled over the rocks. A Pennsylvania Dutch soldier commented that this would be a good place to live and make his home-made beer. Many of the men agreed but they were all happy to just have some cool mountain water and rest.

While they were resting, a man named Roger Johnson, who had been to Fort Ligonier before, told a brief history of it. He was one of the frontier scouts from Bedford who, like Gus, had signed up to help. Several years earlier, he had served with the Pennsylvania militia. He began his story by setting the stage. "It was during the Forbes campaign in the fall of '58 that Colonel Bouquet ordered Major James Grant to build a road from Boswell to Ligonier. The result, as you know, was the road we have been marching on since Bedford. He then sent an engineer named Charles Rohr to the future site to select a location for a storehouse and a fort. When the site was selected, Major Grant, Colonel Burd and 1500 men were sent to begin construction. With them came some of the wives and their children, a few camp followers and a large number of horses, cows, pigs and sheep. Bouquet wanted at least a 120 foot storehouse for supplies and a hospital. While the fort was under construction, Bouquet came to see how things were going only to find that Major Grant had taken a force and headed west to Fort Duquesne. They were beaten by the French, as Sergeant Caldwell has told you. Then came the attack by the French and a few Indians. After the attack, the men continued to build the fort. It survived an attack in 63 by Chief Pontiac and his followers. It now stands ready for any other attack. It was named Ligonier after Sir John Ligonier who is the chief of British forces and military advisor to William Pitt."

After the brief stop was over, the men continued their journey toward Fort Ligonier. The road coming down the mountain was just as bad as the one coming up the other side. Now the men had to be concerned about the wagons tipping over in the ruts or on the sharp turns. The hand brakes they used could only hold back so much, so once again the men were employed to prevent the wagons from getting out of control as they made their way steadily down the steep hillsides. At some points, if they looked over the side of the mountain, they could see for many miles. At other places where the road just cut through the forest, all one could see were trees and undergrowth. The trees here on the west side of the mountain were dense and the laurel that grew here stood five feet tall. The scouts had to be especially careful, for any place along this road could be a good place for an attack. The many crevices, boulders, and fallen trees all could serve as hiding places for the Indians. Captain Barrett became very concerned when they came to a particularly sharp turn in the road that slowed the whole army to a stop and took a half an hour to get one wagon around it safely. So many men were used to control the wagons that it simply seemed like a great place for an attack. He decided that he and his men would backtrack a half a mile east up the mountains and then to make their way slowly westward parallel to the road to see if they had missed any signs. Within fifteen minutes, the scouts came across two Indians watching the progress of the army as it navigated the sharp turn. They were lying behind a log peering down at the scene below them. Using hand signals, Captain Barrett sent his men to surround the Indians, leaving their only escape over the hill into the hands of the army. When the scouts were all in place, they began to slowly close the semi-circle they had made around the Indians who were intent on watching the wagons. The noise of the wagons, soldiers, and teamsters below served to distract the Indians from the little bit of noise the scouts made as they approached from the rear. When they were within twenty five feet of the Indians, Captain Barrett took out his tomahawk. He wanted to try to capture the Indians to get information from them. As the others began to do the same, one man dropped his musket and an Indian heard the noise and looked around. To everyone's surprise, he stood up and charged right into the circle of scouts, his own tomahawk raised high above his head. As he ran, he let out a war cry like Gus had never heard before. But within seconds, he lay on the ground with mortal wounds in his chest. The second Indian, seeing the plight of his friend lifted his musket and took aim at the closest scout. Before he could fire, one of the other scouts threw his tomahawk and hit the Indian on the side of his head. The blow knocked him over and he was immediately overtaken by three other men who picked him up, bound him and checked his wound. He seemed to be stunned, but able to walk, so they marched him off to be interrogated by Colonel Bouquet. The Colonel asked if any of the scouts knew the tribe and language of this Indian. One of the scouts from Cumberland said he was dressed like a member of the Delaware tribe and that he knew enough of their language to get by.

Colonel Bouquet said "Ask him why he was spying on us."

The interpreter did and got no reply.

The Colonel then said, "Ask him how many other Indians are with him spying on us."

The Indian said, "The Indians are all over the forest and you will soon all die."

Then the Colonel asked, "When did the Indians overrun Fort Pitt?"

The Indian replied, "The walls of the fort could not hold them out and that they overran the fort on the first day of the siege. Now, many Indians were waiting to kill all the white soldiers."

Colonel Bouquet knew this was not the case because the Watkins brothers had escaped after the first day of the siege. He assumed this Indian was not telling the truth. He realized that the Indian was a spy whose job it was to report the progress of Bouquet's army back to the main body of Indians who were still near Fort Pitt.

The Colonel told him he was not telling the truth and that he would be locked up at Fort Ligonier for the rest of his days.

As he was being led away, the Indian tripped the soldier and sprang free. He got only a few yards before shots rang out and the second Indian of the day lay dead.

The Colonel ordered all his men to be on alert for they did not know for sure how many Indians were in the woods and if the shots had been heard by others.

The scouts once again mounted the hillside and continued to look for more Indians that might be watching, but they did not come across any and in a few hours all the wagons had made it around the sharp bend and were nearing the gates of Fort Ligonier.

The fort was not much to look at, but it was a welcome sight none-the-less. It was rather rustic, made out of wooden poles and earth. As the men made their way along the south side of the fort, Gus realized that it was shaped much like Fort Bedford. It was a stockade fort with the outer walls made of logs and bundles of limbs tied together. The tops of the logs were pointed and the bottoms were buried deep in the ground. Before an enemy could get to the fort, however, there was an entrenchment all around it and sticking out of the ground was what he had heard someone call an abatis that was made of trees that had been cut down and sharpened on one end facing outward to prevent the enemy from scaling the walls The corners of the fort had triangular shaped points built into the walls in front of the bastions so that the swivel guns mounted there could fire upon the troops that had to run along the base of the fort. Once Gus got inside the fort, he noticed the inner wall that surrounded the two main storehouses. As he looked the fort over, Gus decided that Colonel Bouquet knew a thing or two about warfare and his spirits began to rise a little.

When Colonel Bouquet entered Fort Ligonier, he was welcomed by Colonel James Burd the commander in charge of the fort and the man Bouquet had sent out to build it two years earlier.

"Welcome sir," said Colonel Burd. "I am so happy to see that these two brothers finally made their way to Carlisle and that you have been able to respond so quickly with the supplies and men that our brothers inside Fort Pitt so desperately need."

"Thank you," replied Colonel Bouquet. "We have been pushing ourselves to get here as quickly as possible and will continue to push on until Fort Pitt is relieved. As for the Watkins brothers, they would not take the time off I offered them. I believe they want to be there when we break the siege of those Indians surrounding the fort."

Then Colonel Bouquet asked, "Did the horses I sent arrive safely?"

"Yes, they are penned in a corral. What do you plan to do with all of those horses?"

"Well, sir," said Colonel Bouquet, "I'm going to have all that flour in those big heavy wagons put in sacks and placed on their backs. That way I can move a little faster and not find myself in the same predicament as that fool Braddock was in when he tried to face an enemy that was unencumbered by wagons and cannon."

"So," replied Colonel Burd, "we are beginning to think like the Indians?"

"Yes, to a degree. As an officer, we must know how our enemy thinks and how they will act and then respond to it. I will be ready for their attack in the woods. I plan to relieve Fort Pitt and live to tell about it."

Colonel Bouquet then gave the order to have all of the men rest and eat a good meal. He went off with the officers to the officer's mess where the batmen had prepared a meal of beef, turnips, green beans and corn bread. There was rum for the men and mixed berry pie for dessert.

The troops did not eat as well, but were satisfied with the biscuits and beans. But they, too, had the mixed berry pie, which was a real treat. After their meal the men began unloading the flour from the barrels and putting it in the flour sacks. There were many suspicions about why this transfer was taking place, but nearly everyone knew it was for speed and the Colonel feared attack from the natives, just as Braddock had been attacked as he made his way toward Fort Duquesne years earlier.

Before going to bed, Gus took a look at the armory of the fort. It was amazing. The walls were made of heavy stone and two layers of logs made up the roof. They were then covered with dirt. Grass and weeds were growing on top of that. He doubted that anything or anyone was going to get into it uninvited.

Gus was also impressed with the hospital at the fort. The most common illnesses on the frontier were scurvy or malaria. But the thing he was keenly aware of was what happened to a person who was cut or wounded in battle. Most often, if they survived, they came back to this kind of place and the wounded limb was amputated. He could not imagine how difficult life would be with only one leg or one arm. He quickly put the thought out of his mind and made his way back to his friends who were already sleeping on the ground because the barracks were full. Gus opened his blanket and found a space to lie down. Soon he was asleep.

The next day the men continued to transfer the flour into smaller bags to be carried by the horses. They were done by noon, so after lunch, they were able to relax a bit. No one knew for sure what was in store for them, but they all knew that they had to make it to Fort Pitt and were determined to do so. If they were attacked between Ligonier and Fort Pitt and lost, there would not be another opportunity to mount an offensive before the people at the fort would starve or be compelled to surrender. And if they made it to the fort, and it was still under siege, they knew they would have to fight their way in. No matter how the men looked at it, the next few days were going to be the most important days of the campaign so far.

Since their work was done, Gus and the others had a chance to look around the outside of the Fort. Gus continued to be impressed with how it was built. It seemed to be located in a good spot. It was up on a hillside making anyone who tried to attack it from the west come up the hill. Gus thought that the Army had done a good job in the construction of the two forts he had seen thus far. Though they were rough looking, they were well planned and well situated. He hoped that the Fort in Pittsboro was just as well made so that the people there were still alive.

As he continued to explore, Gus realized that there was great natural beauty in this spot. Just south of the road the army had marched in on was the Loyalhanna creek. Its cool water was used for drinking water by the soldiers at the fort. Gus and his friends filled their canteens there in preparation for the next day's march. The creek was also home to many creatures and served to quench the thirst of many others. The mountains to the east made the sun climb a long way before it peaked over the ridge to bathe the parade ground of the fort. The various trees and shrubs provided a beautiful array of color, from reds to silvers to various shades of green. It was certainly beautiful country. Gus could only imagine what it would look like in the fall when the leaves provided even more colors.

After dinner the men were encouraged to turn in so that they could get an early start the next day. As Gus lay on his blanket under the stars, his thoughts turned to Elizabeth. He desperately wanted to tell her what was in his heart. He wished she were here so they could talk, so he could hold her close one last time. He wanted to tell her he loved her and would be back by her side, but also to admit that he was scared. There among all these men who had been in battle, he felt afraid of how he might perform. He knew that his actions could result in someone else being hurt or killed. There were many emotions, many thoughts that ran through his head as he watched the stars twinkle above him. But the two that brought him calmness were the sights of his dead parents and the comment from Reverend McGregor. He was going to avenge his parents' death and in so doing, impress the good Reverend and his daughter.

CHAPTER NINETEEN

After the Watkins brothers snuck out of Fort Pitt, Captain Ecuyer began to do all he could to shore up the fort and prepare for a long siege. He had food and ammunition, but not an unlimited supply of either. His troops were outnumbered and he had no idea how long the siege would last.

At one point, some of the Delaware chiefs, including Turtle Heart and Natawatwees came to the fort and solicitously suggested that Captain Ecuyer send the women and children back east where they would be safe.

Ecuyer replied, "There is no need for that. As we speak, there are three armies of six thousand men approaching this fort. They will soon be here to send you all running home. When they do get here, they will not stop. They will go to your villages and make war on you and your people. It is you that need to make sure your women, children and old people are safe.

"I have enough food to simply wait here until these armies arrive. And if you try to attack, I am sure you know that you will lose many warriors for nothing. You will never take this fort. It was built to withstand cannon fire. Your arrows and muskets will do us no harm."

Several months went by with no message from anyone back east and no relief force. In the third week of July, the Shawnee Chiefs came to the fort to urge Captain Ecuyer to withdraw. Once again, he said "The British forces are on their way. They will soon be here to end your siege. You need to go back to your warriors and tell them to get ready to die because they surely will."

The next day, the Indians began an attack which would continue for four days and nights. The Indians showed considerable daring as they came to the very edge of the river banks. As a result, seven people in the fort were killed and Captain Ecuyer was himself wounded in the leg. He estimated that twenty Indians were killed in the attack and twice that many wounded.

On August 1, the Indians suddenly ceased their attack. The soldiers and settlers were a bit confused. Captain Ecuyer guessed that the attack was broken off because the Indians had learned of an army approaching. He hoped that was case. He was in desperate need of food and provisions.

He encouraged the soldiers to go out of the fort in small groups and pick whatever vegetables and fruit they could find and bring it back to the fort. The small garden outside the fort was raided at night by the Indians so there was not much left, but the men picked all they could and found berry bushes and fruit trees with ripe fruit. The fresh vegetables gave the people in the fort a bit of a lift. They had been under siege for months. Now there was hope that help was coming.

CHAPTER TWENTY

After breakfast the next morning, Colonel Bouquet called his officers together and said, "Gentlemen, I would like to move as rapidly as possible this morning until we get to the Bushy Run way station that is located nearly half way between here and Fort Pitt. I can tell you from experience that the water there is first rate and plentiful. After a brief rest, we can then time our march through the Turtle Creek defiles to occur at dusk so as to minimize the risk of ambush. Does anyone have any questions?"

None of the men did. They were anxious to get on with the march and the encounter they foresaw in order to save their comrades in arms at Fort Pitt.

Gus and the woodsman scouts led the army out of Fort Ligonier and through the woods, steadily moving westward. Colonel Bouquet gave orders for everyone to pay attention and make as little noise as possible while they made their way. Everyone knew from their earlier encounter that there were probably more Indians lurking in the woods and they grew more fearful with every step they took. They knew that the Indians were not going to simply let them march into Fort Pitt and provide the soldiers with the supplies, cannon and reinforcements they so desperately needed.

Newate was on watch duty when he heard someone walking through the woods. They were walking through the dead leaves and the rustling sound was quite distinguishing against the normal quiet he had grown accustomed to in this place. The noise sounded like only one man, but within a few seconds, it was clear than there were others also walking somewhere nearby. He rushed to get Tamany, but he too had heard the noise and was making his way to where Newate had been hiding. They decided it would be best to hide while they watched to see what was coming down the road. Within a few minutes, the men making the noise had passed them by and out on the main road an army appeared. There were men in a wide variety of outfits and horses caring sacks of something. They estimated that there were three hundred men in all. Tamany was excited because he was sure the Indians surrounding the fort could easily defeat them.

After the army passed by, the Indians decided to run back to Fort Pitt with the news. If they were lucky, they would get back in time to warn the chiefs. They had only run for a few hours when they came upon a large number of Indians coming their way as quickly as they could. The chiefs gathered to hear what news they had to share. Some other scouts had already seen the army making its way to Fort Ligonier. They indicated that there were heavy wagons and about three hundred men. Newate's brother said, "We saw no heavy wagons, but did see many horses caring bags of goods."

The Chiefs decided that the best plan would be to divide their braves into two groups so they could cover either of two roads the approaching army might take as they came west. Once the army was engaged by either group, the warriors who were not in the immediate area would soon be contacted to join in the battle. They hoped to rely on the strategies of former campaigns by creating a net for the white soldiers to walk into. After the fighting would begin, the Indians planned to attack from the front and both sides. They did not want the army to slip through and make its way to Fort Pitt.

It was late morning when the column made the turn off the road that Forbes had built earlier onto the newer South Fork heading towards the Bushy Run outpost.

The outpost had been used by British troops from Fort Pitt and Fort Ligonier to feed and water their horses. As a result, it also became a place to store supplies that were necessary to meet these needs. Over the past few years, civilian travelers would also stop here on their journey to rest before going on. Andrew Barley was the supervisor of the Bushy Run outpost.

While Colonel Bouquet's army was making its way from Ligonier, four Mingo Indians stopped at the outpost to warn those living there to leave the area or they would be killed. Families in the area had been burned out without any warning. Mr. Barely didn't know what to do. He feared for his life, yet, he also had an obligation. He called together his neighbors and told them of the warning. Many already knew about the families that had been burned out. Mr. Barley asked what they wanted to do.

Mr. Gonguware said, "It seems to me if we stick together here we might be better off than running away."

Still others thought that saving their lives by going back east to Fort Ligonier would be better.

Finally, Mr. Barley said, "I'm going to stay here at the station. If any of you would like to join me, you're welcome."

The small community began to make preparations to strengthen the outpost and to bring in supplies of food, gun powder and ammunition that would help them fight off an Indian attack.

While the army marched on, word continued to get back to the Chiefs from other spies they had stationed throughout the forest confirming that a column of militia and British soldiers was approaching. They knew that Fort Pitt had to be reinforced, or it, too, would soon fall. The Indian uprising had already taken the forts at Presque Isle, Le Bouef, and Venango north of Fort Pitt. They knew the importance of the waterways for trade and travel. Fort Pitt controlled both by its location where the Monongahela and Allegheny Rivers met to make to Ohio. The Ohio flowed westward to the Mississippi and then traveled to the great ocean to the south. They believed they had the element of surprise and strength of their side and grew anxious to engage the soldiers and teach them yet another lesson in how to fight in the frontier.

It was August the 5th. Colonel Bouquet and his men knew they had to continue to move on to rescue those trapped at Fort Pitt and so they were marching as quickly as possible. The scouts led the way and were now encouraged to move quickly and carefully at the same time. For Gus and the other scouts, the time was very tense. They had to use all their senses and knowledge of the woods to provide them with any clues regarding the whereabouts of Indians. They were not far from the Bushy Run outpost and that meant, not too far from Fort Pitt. Every step took them closer and closer to the enemy. As they marched along, the conversation stopped. There was none of the normal chatter between the men and everyone became more vigilant. The scouts, along with everyone else, were peering into the woods ahead and on their right and left. The Colonel told them to be alert, to be ready, and so they were.

After a stop for lunch and a brief rest, the Colonel passed the word to move ahead. Most of the men had a drink of water that they had gotten from Ligonier. They had already marched seventeen miles since morning and everyone was tired. Though it was not up hill during this part of the trip, to march that far after the hard march they had already endured had the men worn out. Gus' back hurt and it seemed like he was straining to hear any unusual sound that might alert him to danger. Suddenly the frontiersmen heard the sound of a pheasant taking flight in a small clearing ahead and to their right. That usually meant that the bird had been frightened. They stopped and some of the scouts began to look in that direction. There was a small hill and before long the men noticed some movement, but the figures did not look to be human. In the shadows of the trees were what appeared to be more than simply shadows. After a few seconds, it became clearer that these were men dressed in the briefest attire, but their bodies were painted black and red. The sight of them for the first time made Gus freeze in place and simply stare. He had never seen anything quite like that before and yet there they were, not fifty yards away.

Gus was not sure who fired first, but one of the men from Cumberland yelled for them to open fire and instantly, the muskets were up and firing. Gus, too, took aim at an Indian and pulled the trigger on his musket. For the first time in his life, he suddenly realized, he was aiming at a person with the intention of killing him. It was too late to change his mind. The ball from his musket had already reached its mark, for Gus saw the man stop and fall backward. He did not get back up. Gus wanted to run up to see if he was alive or dead. He thought that maybe he could help him somehow. But just then, a ball tore threw his shirt and cut into the flesh of his left arm. The sting made him realize that he was in the middle of a battle and needed to reload and take aim once again before one of the Indians got a little luckier and his hair ended up on the Indian's belt. He was a good shot, but it still took time to go through all the steps of putting in the power, the cloth, and the ball all while trying not to get shot. At best Gus could only fire twice in a minute. So, in this situation he reasoned, he better make his shots count.

All around Gus white men and Indians were shooting and shouting. The Indians looked like they were from different tribes. They fired their muskets and shot their arrows and then some of them ran at Gus and the others with their tomahawks raised. The sight and sounds made Gus ill. Was this how his mother died? Had someone frightened her and smashed in her head with a tomahawk? It was hard to be brave because Gus had never been in a battle. It was not like hunting deer. The deer never shot back or attacked you.

Beside Gus, one of the men from Virginia was shot in the chest. The blood splattered out onto Gus' face just as he was going through the process of reloading his gun. Before he could stop it, he was bent over throwing up and gagging. He wiped off his face and mouth, but the image could not be wiped out of his mind. Gus tried not to look at the man to his right, but he could not turn away. He just stared at the man next to him with the life slowly pumping out of his chest. Suddenly, a very large Indian ran out of the forest toward him and Gus dropped his gun and picked up the one from the man who was dying beside him. He aimed and fired hoping that the gun was loaded. The Indian was no more that twenty yards away. He wore leather leggings and no shirt. But his face and body were painted somehow in red and black. He had one feather in his hair and he screamed as he ran toward Gus. He had not taken very good aim for the ball hit the Indian in the arm and it did not stop him from his attack. He continued running and Gus screamed in fear. Just then a musket fired from behind Gus and the Indian's face turned red as blood oozed out of the wound just above his right eye. It mingled in with the red and black paint that was on his face. He dropped to the ground not five feet away. Gus turned to see who had saved his life only to find Captain Barrett standing there reloading his musket.

"Reload, Gus," he yelled. "Reload and fire."

The smell of gun powder and the sight of blood, the sound of guns firing and the screams of the Indians, and the moans of people dying all around were nearly too much to bear. Gus just stood there. But Captain Barrett grabbed him by the arm and gave him a quick slap in the face. Finally, Gus responded. He grabbed his own gun and finished placing the powder and ball in the muzzle and began the process of tamping them down. He was not sure if he put in enough powder. Some of it spilled out of his horn, but he finally got done and once again scanned the tree line and the hill top. As he went through this process, more and more Indians became visible. They seemed to be spreading out along the tree line and firing from that vantage point. He almost forgot to put powder in the pan as he lifted his musket up to fire once again.

Captain Barrett encouraged everyone to spread out in a semi-circle and to fire only at what was in front of them. All the men responded by finding a good defensive spot and scanning the area in front of themselves.

"Hold fast men!" he said. "Hold fast!"

The area soon filled up with smoke. It became difficult to see clearly after Gus fired his gun, but in the time it took him to reload, he was able to begin to make out Indians who were shooting muskets or arrows. And even though it made it hard for him to see, Gus reasoned that it probably did the same for the Indians.

Gus watched the tree line in front of him as the Indians moved from one spot to another. He waited for an opportunity to fire as he held his musket up. Musket balls were flying all around him. He decided to seek shelter behind a small oak. It allowed him to fire but provided some protection. Some of the other scouts had already done the same thing. Fighting the way the Indians did seemed to offer a better chance to making it back to his Elizabeth with all his hair.

As he waited to fire, it seemed like there was movement on both sides now. He realized that they had not stumbled upon a small raiding party, but upon a large group of Indians who were intent on not allowing them to get to Fort Pitt.

Before Gus could fire again, Captain Barrett knelt down beside him and said, "Gus, run back to the Colonel and tell him our position and that we need reinforcements."

As quickly as he could, Gus ran away from the smoke, noise and smell of the fighting, but he kept looking over his shoulder, expecting to see one of those red and black men with his tomahawk or musket coming after him. As he ran, several balls struck the trees near him. He heard them thump into the tree trunks. One arrow stuck in the ground just ahead of him. He jumped to his right and kept running as fast as he could. In a few minutes Gus came upon the Highlanders and then Colonel Bouquet. They had heard the shooting and were already making their way to the fighting. Gus told Colonel Bouquet, "Sir, Captain Barrett has sent me to tell you that we have been ambushed."

"How many Indians are there?"

"I don't know, Sir. They are in the trees and brush all around us. Some are up on the hill above us and to our right."

Colonel Bouquet gave the orders for the column to advance, leaving a small group behind to guard the supplies. Gus quickly led the way back to Edge Hill, where the scouts had been ambushed and Colonel Bouquet began to direct the counterattack and to set up a defense. He gave orders for two light infantry companies to dislodge the Indians and they moved forward into the midst of the battle and formed the hollow square from which they could fire from all sides.

Gus ran back to his previous oak tree by Captain Barrett and quickly told him what the Colonel was doing. As he settled into his spot, he noticed that there seemed to be more Indians than before. Again, he watched and waited for an opportunity to fire. He was looking to his left when a ball struck the tree he was using to protect himself just above his head. Gus realized that the ball had come from his right. He fell to the ground and scanned the trees to his right to see who may have fired at him. Then he noticed smoke rising from the end of a musket that stuck out from behind a tree. The musket tilted and he saw an Indian begin to reload the weapon. He had to kneel to get a clear shot, but when the Indian had finished loading and was about to take aim once again, Gus fired and could see the ball strike him in the shoulder. The Indian dropped his weapon and fell to the ground.

Newate felt the sharp pain of the ball as it drove itself into his flesh, through his muscle and smashed against his shoulder bone. He dropped his musket and fell to the ground. He needed to get up, but the pain was great and as he watched his own blood stream out of the wound, the only thing he could do was think about Unamati back in his village and how he might never get to see her again. He took his headband off and tried to tie it around the wound to stop the bleeding, but the task was difficult using only one hand and his teeth. When he had nearly finished, he saw a white man come running at him through the brush. Before he could get up, the man stopped and shouted something at him he did not understand. Newate knew that his life was now over, so he reached for his tomahawk with his left hand and began to stand up to defend himself. As he did so, Gus hit him on the head with his musket and he fell to the ground in a daze.

Without knowing exactly what to do, Gus looked around quickly and discovered some vines, like the ones he used to swing on as a child, hanging from a near-by tree. He quickly cut off some of the vine with his new tomahawk, and then used it to tie the hands and feet of the Indian he had hit over the head. As he tied his feet, Gus noticed the moccasins and the beads sewn into the leggings. He was not sure, but according to what he had been told, this Indian could be from the Delaware tribe like the other two he had already seen. As he rolled him over and looked at his face, Gus realized that this Indian was probably about his own age. It was hard to tell for sure, and at that moment, he was glad he had not killed this person. He began to wonder if he had a mother waiting for his return or a girlfriend or wife in a village somewhere. Gus finished tying the Indian to a tree and once again used another tree to hide behind as he looked for someone to stick their head out for just a bit too long. It only took a few minutes until he found a new target. An Indian fired his musket at another soldier and was just about to kneel back down behind a bush he was using as a hiding place. Gus fired his musket and once again saw the results. The Indian grabbed at his stomach as he fell to the ground.

The men from Cumberland and the Virginia militia fell in line next to the rest of the army and the battle continued. Colonel Bouquet encouraged the men to hold their positions and to fire at only what they could see clearly. He did not want the men to panic, and the classic hollow square had proven to be a well designed means of defense so long as everyone held their place and concerned themselves with what was in front of them.

Captain Charles Lewis was in command of the Virginia militia and he encouraged his men to take aim and hold fast, just as Captain Barrett had his men. These officers seemed to have no fear as they encouraged and gave orders to their men.

The Highlanders in their red coats, stockings and kilts charged after the Indians with their bayonets attached to the end of their muskets. They would regroup, load, fire and then charge ahead to chase the Indians from their hiding places. But it seemed to Gus like no sooner had they been chased from one area than more Indians would show up somewhere else. All the rest of the day, the Indians tested the lines of the soldiers by suddenly attacking in one place and then retreating into the woods. This tactic proved frustrating for the soldiers who were used to men standing in lines across from one another, firing their weapons. It took restraint not to be drawn too far into the woods to chase the Indians down. The Indians were good at ambushes and making one think they had the upper hand only to find themselves cut off from a possible retreat.

The fighting was fierce with many Indians and soldiers losing their lives. It seemed that both sides knew the importance of this battle. If Bouquet and his supplies got through, Fort Pitt would be saved and more settlers would move into the area. If the Indians prevailed, they could starve out those trapped at Fort Pitt and eventually Fort Detroit would also fall and the land would be theirs once again.

As order began to come of the chaos of the first skirmish, Gus looked around at the dead and wounded. He was surprised at how many people lay bleeding on the ground and how many were no longer alive. There must have been thirty or forty soldiers dead and that many or more dead Indians. It was then that Gus remembered the Indian he had shot who was tied up with vines and tied to a tree not far from him. He looked over at the Indian and could see that his shoulder was still bleeding and that he was in a great deal of pain. Gus asked him his name, but the Indian did not respond. Gus yelled over to Captain Barrett who ran to his side. When he got their Gus said, "Captain, I shot this Indian, but he isn't dead. What should I do with him?"

"That's easy," replied Captain Barrett, and he took his tomahawk out of his belt and walked over to the Indian. The man never flinched. He never begged for mercy. He just looked at Captain Barrett and then at Gus. Why Gus yelled out to stop, he didn't know, but his yell got the attention of Colonel Bouquet who also ran over to see what was happening. The Colonel asked who had shot the Indian.

Gus said, "I did, sir."

Then he asked, "Did you tend to his wound too?"

Gus replied, "Yes sir."

"What did you expect to do with him if he lived?" asked the Colonel.

"I don't know, sir, but maybe he could tell us something important."

The Colonel looked at the wounded Indian and told Captain Barrett to keep an eye on him until the battle was over. So Captain Barrett and Gus continued to fight as the Indians continued to appear and disappear behind the trees in front of them.

The afternoon was turning to evening and the Indian attack had slowed down. They were either planning an all out attack before the end of the day or they were withdrawing to prepare to come at the soldiers in the morning. Either way, a pause in the shooting was welcomed by all the men. They began to assess their situation. Most of the men checked their own supplies to see if they needed anything. Then they began to look around for friends to make sure they had lived through the battle.

Colonel Bouquet decided that staying in their current position was not in his best interest. He had been unable to dislodge the Indians and so he gave the order to withdraw about one half-a-mile from Edge Hill to a small clearing. There Bouquet ordered his men to erect an enclosure of flour bags as protection for the wounded. He brought up his supply wagons and that served as his left flank. The rest of the troops formed a circle around the fort.

When the flour bags were piled up, one of the men said, "I never thought I would see a flour bag fort." The comment lightened the mood a little as the soldiers began to bring the wounded inside the newly formed fort. The men who had been shot and still had balls embedded in their bodies were given a drink of whiskey and one of the men who acted as a doctor probed around the hole where the ball had entered the body until he could remove it. Then a hot iron was placed on the wound to stop the bleeding. This same procedure was used on every man who had been shot. Many of the men passed out from the pain. They were taken to a place where they could rest and a bandage was placed over the wound. For those who were cut, but not shot, a bandage was applied and if they could continue the fight, they were sent back out to a post. This is what happened to Gus. The man acting as a doctor poured some whiskey on his wounded arm, wrapped a bandage around it and sent him back out of the fort.

Gus asked Captain Barrett if he could get the man who was removing the balls to take care of the Indian he had shot.

Captain Barrett replied, "He's your Indian. You take care of him."

So Gus scurried over to the Indian brave and lifted him to his feet. He tried to indicate that he had no intention of hurting the Indian, but could not find a way of letting him know that. He just tried to be as gentle as possible with the Indian as he cut the vines from around his ankles. When he brought him into the make-shift fort, some of the men turned to stare. One lifted his musket to fire until he saw that the Indian was tied and bleeding. Colonel Bouquet told Gus to untie him and find someone to take care of the wounded shoulder.

Gus asked the man who was taking out the musket ball from his fellow soldiers if he would remove the one from his Indian captive. The man responded that he would just as soon kill the

Indian as help him. But Gus asked again if he would try to help and the man finally agreed. As the Indian lay on the ground, the man took out a small knife and dug into the shoulder until he hit the ball. Gus held the Indian down so he would not get hurt even worse by jerking. The Indian cried out in pain and passed out as the doctor dug out the ball and handed it to Gus.

"Save it," he said. "You may need to use it again before this is all over."

Gus found some bandages and placed them on the Indian's wound. He once again tied the head band around the shoulder over the bandages and looked again at his Indian. How strange it seemed. He had killed several and now was trying to save one. What an unusual situation he was in. Gus left him there in the fort with the other wounded.

Chief Natawatwees had not seen his youngest son for some time, but he was sure that he was with his brothers and that they would keep him safe. When they all began to gather by Bushy Run Creek for a drink and something to eat, he asked if anyone had seen his son Newate. One of the braves from his tribe said, "I saw Newate get shot by a white man and fall to the ground."

Chief Natawatwees asked, "What happened next? Did he get up? Did anyone help him?" The brave told him that he had not seen any more than what he had just reported. The boy had been shot and fallen to the ground. Natawatwees walked away from the others and began to sing a song for this dead son.

Throughout the Indian camp, many other braves were looking for their friends or relatives. After a while they got together in tribal groups and each tribe mourned the deaths of their braves. Many men had died that afternoon and many more were wounded. Some of the men tended to the wounded. Some stood guard. Some began to rest to prepare for the next day and the next battle.

In and around the flour bag fort, the men were given something to eat and drink. The water that remained was used spar ingly. Gus and the other soldiers ate the bread that was issued to them. It was made of flour and was very hard. The soldiers usually soaked it in warm water until it was soft enough to chew but today they did not have enough water to spare. The Army made the bread this way so it would last for a very long time before spoiling. They were also given pork that had been cut into chunks and soaked in salt water so it wouldn't spoil. Gus and the others boiled dry beans with their meat. After cooking a long time, the beans became soft and the meat less salty. The result was a tasty stew. Everyone was hungry and the meal was most welcome. Gus realized when he got his food just how hungry he was. It did not take him long to clean his plate.

After everyone had eaten, Colonel Bouquet called his officers together and said, "I am so proud of you and your men. I believe we have held off a force of five hundred Indians. Please tell your men that I appreciate the way they behaved themselves while under attack. On another occasion, not so long ago, I was with an army that was defeated in a similar ambush."

All of the officers knew he was talking about Braddock's defeat that took place not too far from where they were fighting. They too were glad that this first battle had not ended the same way. The Colonel ordered the officers to have their men move out in battalions to surround the hilltop where the Indians remained. Guards were posted within each battalion and the officers began to select men to take turns on watch. Gus was not ordered to stand guard at the beginning of the shift. He was told to try to get some rest. Everyone knew that the next day would be just the same as this one had been, or perhaps even worse.

Colonel Bouquet wrote to General Amherst that evening. Part of the letter said, "We expect to begin at daybreak. Whatever our fate may be, I thought it necessary to give your Excellency this early information." He went on in the letter to commend his men for their "Cool and steady behavior."

Gus, like many of the men, had not had an opportunity to relieve himself since the battle began. He made his way to a small shrub and began to go when he suddenly remembered his Indian captive. This man had had no food or water and no opportunity to relieve himself either. Gus began to feel sorry for the man, but then he quickly changed his mind and imagined how many white settlers or trappers he might have killed. He was obviously too young to have been the one who killed his parents, but he could have killed others. He was torn about what to do. He should at least offer him some water. Gus decided to ask Captain Barrett what he should do.

The Captain was talking to some of his men as Gus came up and waited for an opportunity to speak. When he did he said, "Sir, I want to thank you for saving my life today. I believe I was frozen there and that Indian would have surely killed me."

"No need to thank me, Gus, just be sure to pick up the gun next time and fire. Besides, you're the one who ran to get help and probably saved many scalps this afternoon."

"Speaking of scalps, sir", said Gus, "would it be alright if I gave that Indian a drink of water?"

"No," said Captain Barrett. "He can swallow his spit."

"Yes, sir." said Gus, "but can I take him over to relieve himself?"

"What are you Gus, an Indian lover? Didn't you hear any of the stories that were told on the way over here? These men are savages and murders. Do you think he would be looking after you if the tables were turned? No! He would have killed you and taken your hair while you were still bleeding. Let him go on himself for all I care."

Gus went over near the Indian and sat with his back against the wall. He pulled his hat down over his face and tried to get some sleep. As he closed his eyes, he saw Elizabeth in her long pink dress she liked to wear with her black shoes. She often wore a bonnet that covered up her brown curly hair. The thing he liked the most about her was her eyes. They were blue and soft, even when she was angry like when he told her he had joined up with the soldiers. The rest of her body was rigid as he recalled with her hands on her hips, but her eyes were soft even then. How he wished he could be back with her now. But if he made it through this fight, he would go back a hero. That would show her father. That would prove that he was worthy. He fell asleep with the vision of her smiling eyes and was more determined than ever to make it home again.

CHAPTER TWENTY-ONE

Gus was awakened by a soldier who had been on watch. He told him that it was his turn and Gus was directed to go to a spot not too far from where he had been sleeping. Gus got up and stretched. He grabbed his gun and bag with the balls and powder and made his way to the spot. It was still dark and the stars were very bright. Though there were others on guard, no one was talking. Gus could hear the sound of men sleeping. Some of them snored. Others mumbled in their sleep. His thoughts turned to Elizabeth once again. He knew she was safe at the fort and began to imagine her mumbling or snoring. That thought made him smile and he gazed up into the stars to find the constellations he knew and to wonder about the vastness of the night. He had been taught that God created the heavens and the earth. He wondered if God was out there somewhere. If God was out there, did He care one way or another about this battle? If God created everything, did he create the Indians? If he did, then whose side was He on? Gus reasoned that most of the Indians didn't believe in God so even if He created them, the white men had to be His favorites in the rest of this battle. Then he prayed that he was right. He followed that with the Lord's Prayer and the 23rd Psalm he had learned as a child. When he got to the part about walking through the valley of the shadow of death, he suddenly stopped. This must be what the person who wrote it had in mind. He certainly was closer to death now than he had ever been. He continued "I will fear no evil, for thou art with me. Thy rod and thy staff will comfort me all the days of my life, and I shall dwell in the house of the Lord forever." It gave Gus some comfort to pray but when he was done he checked his musket, tomahawk and knife to make sure he was ready for what everyone knew was coming at first light.

As the sky began to brighten in the east, the birds began to awaken and sing their morning songs. Robins, black birds, bob whites, sparrows and even a turkey could be heard. They sang and called and seemed to be delighted that a new day had begun. The singing of the birds and the morning light woke up some of the men. They did not seem to be delighted. It only took a few seconds for them to remember their circumstances and even some of their friends who had died just the day before.

As the men got up, they checked their weapons as Gus had done and made sure they had enough ammunition to fire at the Indians they knew would be attacking. As the sky lightened, the men could see more clearly into the woods around them. They were grateful that the Colonel had decided to move to the clearing to give them some space to see the enemy coming. This small advantage seemed to give the men some courage as they stood ready to face the uncertainty of the new day.

Chief Natawatwees and the Delaware braves with him rose early that day. They ate breakfast. Theirs was dried deer meat that had been made into a jerky. They also picked some of the black-berries that were growing on the bushes next to the creek. The leaders of all of the tribes met to decide what they would do to win the battle that day. It was decided that they would do what had worked so many times before against the British. They would approach them from the woods in the front and on both sides. They would hope to kill as many as possible by staying behind trees. If the British tried to escape out the back, they would continue to circle around and kill them as they fled the fort they had made. The Indians were great in number and were confident that they would kill these men and stop the British from coming into the Ohio Valley for good.

As they prepared for battle, the Indians checked their supplies. The muskets they had taken from the British Forts they had overrun gave them the same kind of weapons as the British were using. They had the ammunition to go with them and so they were ready for this battle. Those who had no musket had bows and arrows. These were weapons that were quite accurate for short distances and the bow could be reloaded with another arrow nearly every five seconds. Depending on where the arrow struck, they could be just as damaging as a musket ball.

With the chiefs in the lead, the Indians made their way to the woods surrounding the flour bag fort. These woods were dense with oak, chestnuts, hickory, and pine trees. They met briefly with the men who had been left on guard to see if the soldiers had made any changes. After they got their report, the Indians moved out to their predetermined areas and began to approach the soldiers' position for the day's battle. As they moved closer, Chief Natawatwees kept one eye on the flour bag fort ahead and one eye on the ground looking for the body of his dead son. He was determined to make some white man pay for his death.

At first light, Colonel Bouquet gathered his officers and told them that they had to keep control of their men and help them to remain calm, no matter what happened. He knew that if the men began to panic under the attack, it would be infectious and all would be lost. He needed all of his men waiting for a good shot and making their shots count.

Captain Barrett came over to where his men from Cumberland were gathered. Gus had been with them from the time they came to Fort Bedford. He had gotten to know some of the men pretty well. He knew that before the day was over, some of these men would be dead. Perhaps he too would be dead. The thought made the breakfast turn over in his stomach.

Captain Barrett was saying, "Men, we need to fight smart today. Fight smart. Take a shot when you can, and for God's sake, don't run away at the first sign of an Indian feather."

Some of the men chuckled. Many of them had a long history with Indians. Some of it was good, some of it, not so good. But none of them were afraid of a fight. They were men like Gus, but just a little older.

"Now, be at the ready men and make me proud." said Captain Barrett. "Let's show these Indians what we're made of."

It didn't take long before Gus and the others saw movement once again in the woods in front of them. The officers saw it too and ordered the men to hold their fire until they had a good shot. Everyone was becoming anxious and more than one man wet himself as a sudden explosion of musket fire came from the woods as if on command. Balls came flying at the men from all directions. The soldiers were ordered to fire in return and soon the sound of gunfire was deafening. Gus saw an Indian get shot in the stomach and the man beside him yelled for joy.

"I got him!" he said. "I got one of them Indians! And if I live, I'll scalp him and turn it in."

More and more Indians seemed to be coming to the woods right in front of Gus and the scouts from Bedford and Cumberland. They began to move from tree to tree, closer to their position. All of the soldiers were shooting as quickly as they could reload, and Indians were falling dead or wounded, but so were some of the soldiers.

Captain Lewis and Captain Barrett were encouraging their men to take aim and to not be afraid. It gave Gus some courage that he was not sure he would have had otherwise.

Chief Natawatwees urged his braves onward. They were right in the thick of things and taking some losses, but he was determined to win this battle. His other sons were mixed in with the tribe, but he called for them to come to his side. "I do not want to lose another son." he said. "Fight by me so we can protect each other and kill these white men."

Glikikan was making his way over to him; he left the cover of the trees. Gus saw the Indian running in front of him and fired at him. The ball from his musket pierced the Indian's thigh and he fell to the ground. From where he lay, the Indian was exposed to more fire and Gus reloaded his musket to shoot him once again, but other Indians ran to his rescue. As they bent to pick him up, one of them was shot in the back.

Chief Natawatwees ran out and helped Tamany who had run out to get his younger brother who Gus had shot in the thigh. The three of them hid behind a large pine tree and cut Glikikan's leggings open with a knife, quickly dug out the ball, tied a band around his leg and propped him up against the tree to rest. He was left with his musket and tomahawk to protect himself in the event the battle did not turn out as they expected, but his father assured him that they would be back. The Chief was so angry, he could not be stopped. He rallied his warriors and their attack became even more furious.

Colonel Bouquet noticed heavy fire coming from the place where the Delaware were attacking. He was concerned that his men may not be able to hold out there much longer, but he thought that if he sent reinforcements to that spot, the Indians would attack another area where it was weakened. He nonetheless did reinforce with a few men and the battle continued on. Heavy fighting took place and losses continued to mount for both sides. Finally, Colonel Bouquet gathered his officers once again and told them of a plan that he had. He would pull back his men from the side where the fighting was the fiercest and make it look like they were collapsing. When the Indians saw this, he hoped that they would respond by rushing into the space where the lines had been.

Captain Barrett came back to his men and told some of them to slip back into the ranks of the other soldiers on either their left or right one at a time so as not to be noticed. Little by little it looked like the ranks were thinning. Captain Lewis' company was ordered to do the same. Finally, Captain Barrett ordered Gus and the remaining men to pull back to the center of the hollow square to shorten their lines. The men began to wonder what Colonel

Bouquet was up to, but they obeyed the order and moved back as if in retreat.

When Chief Natawatwees and the other Indians saw the line collapse, they thought that the British were on the verge of defeat and began to rush out from behind the trees to attack the fort. He encouraged his braves and ran before them to lead the way. White men would die this day. But just as they rushed toward the center of the lines that had just moved back, Colonel Bouquet ordered his men on the right flank to quickly out- flank the Indians. As they completed this flanking maneuver, the men were able to fire at the Indians, cutting them down with their musket balls as they ran from their hiding places and then rushing upon them with their bayonets. The Indians fought bravely, but they were now being fired on from the front and the side and they had left the protection of their trees. Then Bouquet sent out his left flank and the Indians were caught in between the soldiers in front of them and those now on both sides.

The Indians were taken by surprise. Chief Natawatwees and Tamany began to look around for a way to escape the trap they had rushed into. Those who continued the attack toward the fort were shot at by Gus and the men who soon retook their places.

Gus noticed that one of the Indians was a large young man, dressed much like the others, but he had a long scar across his face. Gus could see his eyes and they declared his determination to kill someone. He ran forward with tomahawk raised, screaming at the top of his lungs a war whoop that froze Gus in his place momentarily. But just as the Indian was about to smash Gus' head in, he raised his musket and put a ball into the right side of the man's chest. The Indian tried to continue his charge, but he finally stumbled and fell just in front of Gus. He did not move again. The rest of the Indians realized that they had only one option. They had to run for their lives back into the woods. But as they began to do so, Colonel Bouquet sent two more companies out to block their escape. The flanking procedures had broken off the Indian attack and now they were beginning to prevent them from escaping. Chief Natawatwees decided it was better to run away and save his life and that of his wounded son than to die with honor in this place. He yelled for his braves to retreat back into the woods. At this point, it was every man for himself. The Indians ran just to save their lives. As they ran off, Colonel Bouquet sent the men from Virginia and from Cumberland to hunt them down and kill as many as possible.

Chief Natawatwees ran to the pine tree where his son was sitting. He grabbed him under his arm and began to run as quickly as he could to get away from the advancing white men. Gun shots rang out and balls slammed into the trees around them as they hurried through the trees and shrubs. They were determined to get away, but running with a son that could only hop on one leg was slowing them down. When they came to a pine grove, Chief Natawatwees and Glikikan decided to crawl into the grove and hide. The ground was soft with pine needles so they lay there trying to catch their breath. His son asked Chief Natawatwees where his older brother was, but the Chief did not know.

He told him, "When we charged the white men he was by my side, but when they outflanked us, everyone began to run for their lives. I only hope that he is alright. We will meet up with all our warriors later and I am sure we will see him there."

Very soon, however, they heard voices of the white men searching the forest. The Chief peered out through the branches and saw men dressed in deerskin. These were not the men in the red coats. They were frontiersmen who knew how to hunt. He began to become concerned for his life and that of his son. But the men seemed to be in a hurry and were not reading the signs very well. They were simply chasing his warriors and trying to kill as many as they could as they ran off. The whole situation made Chief Natawatwees angry. He should not have listened to Pontiac. He should not have encouraged his tribal leaders. He should not have let his youngest son come to this place. And he should not have run into the trap the white men had set for him. He decided then and there that he would have nothing more to do with these white men and that he would stay away from them and their forts. He just wanted to go back home to his wife and lead a normal life once again. He had lost a son, maybe two, and here he was hiding with a third who had been shot. He did not know how many of his tribe had been killed, but he knew that he had had enough of this battle and wanted to get away as quickly as he could.

After a short while, the shooting ceased. The battle was over. Gus and the other men slowly returned to the flour bag fort and began to reassemble. The death and devastation was all around. Gus looked around as he made his way through the battlefield and it seemed to him like there were more dead men today than there were yesterday. He noticed one drummer and several other members of the Highlanders lying on the ground. It reminded him of the story of Fort Duquesne and what the Indians had done to the Highlanders there. Besides the dead, there were nearly as many wounded. These thoughts of dead and wounded brought his mind back to his Indian. He wondered how he was holding up. He had had nothing to eat or drink since yesterday and there he sat, tied up, unable to move. When Gus got back into the fort, their eyes met. He must have known that the soldiers had won this battle. The shooting was over and people were giving each other slaps on the back while others tended to the wounded. Despite what Captain Barrett had said, Gus got the remaining water from his canteen and took it to the captive Indian to drink. At first, the Indian refused, but finally he drank all that was left.

Captain Lewis and his men from Virginia were chasing down Indians and had nearly decided to return to the battlefield when he noticed what looked like a small group of Indians up ahead. He encouraged his men to hurry, so they ran to catch up with the Indians. When they were nearly upon them, the men stopped, took aim and opened fire. Several Indians fell and when they did, the soldiers realized that the group they had chased was not all Indians. It looked like they were taking a group of prisoners back to their village. The Indians responded by prodding the prisoners to run along the paths in front of and behind them so as to shield them from any further attack. Captain Lewis was compelled to hold his fire while he and the men from Virginia tried to close the gap between them and the Indians ahead.

As the woods thickened again, the militia became more cautious. Their pace slowed even more and they began to look closely into the trees and underbrush, fearing another ambush. Within a few minutes, shots rang out again. A new skirmish was on. Indians had lined both sides of the trail and were firing from behind the trees. Unlike the Highlanders, the militia did not chase after them into the woods to kill them with the bayonets attached to the end of their rifles. Instead, they began to fight back as they had the first day of the battle by taking cover and waiting for an Indian to rise up to take a shot or watching for the smoke and fire that came out the end of a musket barrel. Now the men took better aim and began to pick off the Indians one by one until only a few were left. Seeing that they too were about to be killed, the remaining Indians who had been guarding the prisoners quickly let them go and ran off in different directions deeper into the forest.

When the shooting stopped, the soldiers called out to those they had seen with the Indians and assured them that it was safe to come out of the woods. In a few minutes, they heard the sound of people making their way through the bushes toward them. They remained on guard until they saw that the people coming toward them were actually women and girls. They had been tied together so they could not run away and came out of the forest onto the path one at a time, still tied like a line of pack horses. The soldiers quickly untied the ladies and offered them water from the few canteens they had with them. By the time everyone had come out of the woods, they counted forty women and children in the group they had rescued. One of those rescued was Mary McCord from Chambersburg. There were also three little girls who were sisters. Their names were Mary, Jane and Susan Lowry.

Captain Lewis talked to the ladies for a few minutes and explained who they were and what had just happened. Then he told them that he was going to take them back to the battlefield where they would be safe. He asked if they could all walk and they said that they could, so Captain Lewis and the militia escorted the forty people who had been taken from their homes back to Colonel Bouquet. As they walked, some of the women began to cry, remembering what had happened to their families or just out of gratitude for being safe and free once again.

Colonel Bouquet ordered a burial detail and many men began the gruesome job of identifying and burying their friends. He also sent a company on to the Bushy Run outpost to see if the people who were there were alright. It was only a mile away and everyone feared it had been destroyed. When the men got to the outpost, it was still intact. But it looked like it had been attacked as there were many holes and marks in the door and boards that were over the windows. The lieutenant in charge called out to the outpost to see if anyone would respond. Soon there was a reply and the voice asked who was calling them. The Lieutenant identified himself as Lieutenant Jonathan Scott of the Royal Highlanders. Then the people in the outpost quickly opened the door and welcomed the soldiers.

Mr. Barley said, "We were warned to leave, but did not. Then yesterday we saw hundreds of Indians hurrying by. They did not pay too much attention to us. Then we heard the gun fire and feared that the army we had heard was coming had been ambushed. When we woke up to more gunfire today, we were encouraged. But not long ago a group of Indians came by and nearly shot and hacked their way into this place. We fought them off and they resisted very little. They must have been on the run from you fellas." The Lieutenant told him about the two days that he and the others had fought the Indians and how they had run off in all directions not long ago. He also indicated that there were many wounded and asked if there was water and bandages that could be used to help them. Mrs. Barley, Mrs. Gonguware and some of the other women agreed to start making bandages and told Lieutenant Scott to bring the wounded to the outpost.

While some of the men were digging the holes for burial and others were gone to the outpost, Colonel Bouquet called his officers together and congratulated them on their victory. But it had been a costly victory and he was not sure the fighting was over. For now it seemed the Indians were gone, but one never knew where they might pop up next and they had to be prepared. He decided to keep the majority of the men inside the fort for a while to rest and tend to the wounded. If men did go out, they went in large groups.

Chief Natawatwees and his son waited until they could no longer hear any of the white soldiers and slowly made their way out from under the pine trees. The Chief once again acted as a support for the son who Gus had shot in the leg. As quickly and quietly as they could, they began to make their way away from the soldiers. They walked along keeping the setting sun in front of them. The sun would take them home to the Ohio territory and away from these white men.

When Lieutenant Scott returned from the outpost, he reported to Colonel Bouquet. The Colonel decided to have all the wounded moved to the outpost to receive treatment by the women there. Most of the wounded had been shot but a few had been struck by arrows and others cut by tomahawks. If the men could walk, they were encouraged to do so. Those who could not walk were carried by others the mile to the outpost.

Just after they left, Captain Lewis came through the forest into the clearing and surprised everyone with the forty ladies and girls. Colonel Bouquet went over quickly to meet them and to spare them the horror of seeing so many dead bodies. But one of the teenage girls saw an Indian dead and she walked over to the body and spit on it. One of the ladies went to her and held her close. The sight nearly brought tears to many of the men. They could only imagine what the Indians had done to these people and they did not like what came to mind.

Colonel Bouquet decided to send the ladies and girls to the outpost along with the wounded. He reasoned that they may be helpful or maybe, the ladies at the outpost may help them. He was not sure what he would do with them next, but for now having them at the outpost instead of at this battlefield seemed to make more sense. Captain Lewis and his men then took the ladies to the outpost and tried to find out who the people were, where they had lived and how long they had been prisoners. The more they chatted, the more the ladies opened up. The soldiers shared some of their jerky and talked about their families if they had any. It was a time of healing for the ladies.

CHAPTER TWENTY-TWO

When Captain Lewis returned to the battlefield, he gave Colonel Bouquet a list of names of the ladies and what town each had lived in when they were taken by the Indians. Colonel Bouquet sent two of his men back to Fort Ligonier to let them know of the ambush, to share the news about the rescue and to pass on his letters to Amherst. The men were given supplies and instructions to be careful because no one knew for sure if there were more Indians lurking in the woods. The men that were selected were two scouts from Virginia. Gus wished for a moment that he had been one of them.

As the Colonel made the rounds of the flour bag fort talking briefly to the men, he came upon Gus and his wounded Indian. Somehow, in the midst of the battle, everyone had forgotten about Gus' Indian. But now, the Colonel was curious.

"What tribe is he from?" he asked Gus.

"I don't know for sure," said Gus, "but I think he is Delaware."

Captain Barrett came over and agreed with Gus. The Colonel asked to have the scout from Cumberland who had interpreted for the Indian captured outside of Ligonier try to communicate with the Indian.

The Colonel asked, "What is your name?"

The man asked and Newate told him. "Newate."

"Are you a Delaware?"

The man asked and Newate said, "Yes."

The Colonel asked where he came from.

The man asked and Newate told him, "From the Ohio Territory."

"How many warriors were with you?"

When the man asked, Newate replied "500".

When the Colonel had the man ask about Fort Pitt, Newate did not respond. The Colonel thought that he was withholding information that may save lives and so he drew his sword and placed the point of it on Newate's chest while the man ask the question again. Newate again showed no fear but finally told the Colonel through the interpreter that he and the others had been at the fort on the rivers and that most had left to come here to fight him.

For his cooperation, Colonel Bouquet told Gus, "Give him something to eat."

The Colonel decided that he was going to have Gus hang onto this Indian until they got to Fort Pitt. He might come in handy if he encountered any more hostiles.

Gus got some meat from the cook and brought it back to Newate. He had to cut the vine off his hands so he could eat, but the Indian made no attempt to do anything but eat the meat. He looked at Gus while he ate and there seemed to be sadness in his eyes, as if to communicate that he had failed somehow. Gus got him some water and Newate drank it all again and seemed grateful, though no words were spoken.

The two men Colonel Bouquet had sent to Fort Ligonier hurried back the same way they had come just two days earlier. They were careful to move quickly and not make noise. Though they believed they had sent the Indians back to the Ohio Territory, they were not sure and so they were quiet and careful as they made their way along the trail. They slept overnight off the side of the trail and did not light a fire or make coffee; instead, they ate dried jerky and some apples they found under a nearby tree.

The next day they arrived again at Fort Ligonier. Colonel Burd met with the men and received their report. He shared the good news with the officers and then with all of the men at the fort.

He said, "Men, I have news to share. These brave gentlemen have just told me that Colonel Bouquet was ambushed near the Bushy Run outpost."

The men in the fort felt sick with this news. They had just seen all those men a few days before.

Then he added, "Even though he was outnumbered, Colonel Bouquet outwitted those foxes and showed them the sharp end of a 'Brown Bess' bayonet."

The men let out a cheer and began to slap each other on the back with joy.

"The best part is that while under attack, Bouquet used all those damn bags of flour he was hauling to Fort Pitt as shelter!"

Again the cheers went up, along with some laughter, as the men remembered the flour being transferred to bags for the pack horses.

"And now, gentlemen," continued Colonel Burd, "Colonel Bouquet and his men are pressing on to Fort Pitt!"

Once again the cheers went out and soon the whole fort began to celebrate. Although they had not been under siege themselves, they had been attacked several years earlier while the fort was being built, and they feared that if Fort Pitt fell, they would be next.

"Finally," said Colonel Burd, "after the battle, Captain Lewis of the Virginia militia and his men rescued forty women and girls that the Indians had as prisoners. I have a list of their names and I will have it posted. I'm sure that Colonel Bouquet will come back this way after he has fulfilled his mission. If you know any of these people or their families, let them know to be ready to welcome home these who were taken by the Indians. I am so glad for this news and for this rescue. Thank God Almighty for this glorious victory!"

After the celebration including the first good meal the men had eaten since they left Fort Ligonier, Colonel Burd provided the two men Bouquet had sent with more provisions and two additional men to accompany them back to Fort Bedford and eventually on to Major-General Amherst. Three days later the men arrived at Fort Bedford and met with Lieutenant Carree.

They retold the story of the ambush and how Bouquet had out-witted the Indians. The Lieutenant was excited to hear the news about the victory and the freedom of the women. He ordered a hot meal for the men so they could relax and retell the whole story with all of the details for all the officers in the fort. Finally, when the retelling was over, one of the officers asked about some of the men from Bedford who had signed up to go with Colonel Bouquet. Then one of the men remembered that Gus was the one Captain Barrett had asked to run to get the Colonel and that he had shot the Indian he had all tied up in the flour bag fort. This brought on a mixture of cheers and laughter. Some of the men knew Gus' parents and most knew the story of their death. It was hard for them to figure out why Gus had not just killed the Indian. None the less, he was a hero and everyone raised their cups to Gus, a brave sixteen year-old who was out fighting Indians. The other man also remembered that Gus had been wounded and patched up after the first skirmish. Everyone agreed that he was lucky it was only a flesh wound and he was brave to go back into battle; they drank to their hometown boy once again. "Oh, yes," the first man commented once again, "and I saw him shoot one of those big Indians right in the chest. He fell dead within a few feet of where we were standing." And once again cheers went up for Gus and the other brave soldiers.

Word of Colonel Bouquet's victory soon spread throughout Fort Bedford and into the village. Everyone was glad that Gus had survived the battle and they each had a theory on why he had tied up the Indian he had shot. One man thought he was just too scared to finish him off, but then he was told about the Indian he had killed. Another thought maybe he was going to bring him back to kill him at his parents gravesite. Finally, someone thought maybe he felt sorry for the Indian.

When Elizabeth heard the news, her heart leapt in her chest. She had been expecting to hear that he had been killed. Every day she prayed for him. It was so hard not being able to talk to him or see him. She felt the same way about Gus as Gus did about her. Their friendship had turned into love and she was nearly out of her mind not knowing where he was or if he was safe. What a relief it was to know that he was fine. She breathed a sigh of relief for just a second and then began to wonder where he would go next and what danger might be still out there waiting for her boy, no, her man. Would there be more Indian attacks as he went to Fort Pitt? What did he plan to do with the Indian he had shot? Oh, how she wished she could just talk to him. No, she wished she could hold him and maybe share a real kiss and not just a peck on the cheek. In spite of what her father thought, Elizabeth's heart belonged to Gus and she could wait for him to return.

CHAPTER TWENTY-THREE

The day after the battle at Edge Hill near Bushy Run, Colonel Bouquet called together all the men who could travel and fight and said, "Men, you did a fine job yesterday. We were outnumbered, but you did not run. You fought hard and distinguished yourselves. I am proud of your victory."

The men responded with a cheer.

After they got quiet again, Colonel Bouquet said, "I do not know what awaits us between here and Fort Pitt. But I am determined to relieve that fort and save the people there if there are any still alive. We only have twenty five miles to go men. As soon as we finish eating, we need to pack up and move out for Fort Pitt."

Gus and the others ate a breakfast of biscuits, ham, eggs and coffee. The people who had taken refuge at the outpost returned to their farms and brought back these special items as a way of saying thank you to Colonel Bouquet and his men. After breakfast the men made sure they had enough powder, and balls for their muskets. They got what additional supplies they needed, filled their canteens with the cool, good water from the stream at Bushy Run and were soon ready to move out once again.

Some of the wounded were placed in wagons, some on litters. Most of them walked with bandages over their wounds. Gus walked with the wounded and his Indian. The women at the outpost had made a sling for the Indian's arm that held it up some; this seemed to help with the pain. Gus tied a rope around his waist and attached it to a wagon, but it did not seem like the Indian was in a hurry to try to escape. They were at the back of the line and it was not nearly as much fun as it was up in the front.

As they started out, one of the men Gus had gotten to know from the first part of the trip asked him, "Gus, what are you going to do with that Indian?"

"I don't know yet," replied Gus, "but the Colonel told me to keep an eye on him until we can figure something out."

"You better keep both eyes on him to make sure he does not take your scalp," replied the man.

All the wounded fellas laughed at that, and even Gus had to smile a little.

The march to Fort Pitt went slowly. Colonel Bouquet decided to take all the wounded he could as well as the women and girls who had been prisoners with him to the fort. The result was that the march was slow and the stops were frequent. Colonel Bouquet felt like he had to take everyone to a place that was safe and where there was shelter for his men to heal and the women to feel secure. He did not know for sure what the Indians might try to do as he approached the fort, so after the stop for lunch, the women and the wounded were placed in between the two outer lines that walked on both sides of the road. The scouts up front under Captain Barrett's command were very cautious. The enemy had not all been killed, but they had dispersed. That simply meant they were out there somewhere.

As they marched along, the scouts spread out and traveled as they had before in pairs or small groups along the many paths and trails that ran east and west parallel to the road. They discovered many signs that the Indians had retreated along these trails. Blood was spotted frequently indicating that some of the men were wounded. And at least six Indians who had died from their wounds were discovered. One of the scouts came across an Indian who had been left behind. He had been shot in the stomach and he was near death. When the scout approached, the Indian fired his musket, but he missed the soldier. The sound brought others running to the spot and one of the men asked the Indian what tribe he was with and where his village was. The Indian would not respond. Seeing his condition and his unwillingness to be of any assistance, some of the men wanted to put a musket ball into his head. Others just wanted to leave him to his misery. In the end, that opinion won over. The rational was, "Why waste a ball on an Indian that was already nearly dead?" The scout who had found him took his French musket, his tomahawk and his bag of powder and ammunition then left the man to die.

At the end of the first day, the army set up camp using the supply wagons to form a square and putting the wounded inside. Though all the scouting reports indicated that the Indians had not stopped anywhere that they could see, Colonel Bouquet was very cautious. Being just one day's march away, he did not want to take any chances with his supplies or his new responsibility of these women and girls.

Somehow, even though there was tension in the air about the previous battle and the men who had been lost, there was also a different feel among the troops. Perhaps it was confidence. Maybe it was anticipation. Or, it may have just been those women in camp who seemed to change the atmosphere completely. Gus saw how gentle they were with the young girls and some of the men whose bandages they changed. He was reminded of his mother and he became angry once again at the Indians who had killed so many people like his parents. Then he looked at his Indian captive and wondered what he had been thinking about when he tied this one up instead of just shooting him in the head. There was no answer.

As the evening grew into night, Gus found Sergeant Caldwell and as they sat around the fire, Gus told him the story of how he had found his parents dead in their cabin. The Sergeant replied, "I was wondering what would make a nice young fella like you sign up to be a scout. I suppose that would do it."

Then Gus said, "I made two promises in Bedford. The first was to get revenge for their deaths. I know for sure that I killed two Indians and wounded two more. I suppose that makes me even."

"It might," said the Sergeant, "if you hadn't saved the one Indian's life. Why'd you do that Gus?"

"I don't know for sure," Gus replied, "But I guess I figured he could give us some information, and he already has. Besides, killing a wounded man is different than killing a wounded deer."

"What was the second promise?" inquired the Sergeant.

"To earn the respect of a man who thinks you have to be educated to be worthy of his daughter's hand." said Gus.

"Oh, so there is a girl in your life?" said Sergeant Caldwell with a smile.

"Yes," said Gus, "her name is Elizabeth and she is very pretty."

"I'm sure she is. Now while you are out there seeking revenge and respect, remember to keep your head down. It will do you no good to be a hero if you are dead."

"Thanks. I'll remember the advice."

The next morning, the army was ready to begin their final march to Fort Pitt. The mood was a little tenser now.

One of the scouts said, "Them Indians know where we are. If they are going to stop us, today will be the day."

Everyone agreed. But the general feeling was that they had beaten them once and they could do it again. They just hoped that there were no more Indians waiting near the fort than had met them at Bushy Run.

Gus asked Captain Barrett if he could have one of the wounded soldiers look after his Indian while he joined the scouts once again. His arm was feeling better and he wanted to be as useful as possible. The Captain agreed and Gus moved out with the scouts as they led the way in the final leg of the march to Fort Pitt.

Near mid-day, the scouts were making their way over a high hill. Someone noticed the river off to their left. The older men identified it as the Monongahela River. That meant that the fort was not too far away. Captain Barrett stopped and let the main body of the army catch up to him. Colonel Bouquet called for his telescope that he used to look along the banks of the river and off in the distance toward Fort Pitt. There were no obvious signs of Indian encampments, but still he wanted to be cautious.

The scouts moved out once more, this time looking for any sign that the Indians were still in the area. As they fanned out, Gus came across the remains of a camp site. There had obviously been a campfire here. The grass and shrubs were worn down around the camp site. It may have been a place where the Indians camped during the siege. Gus called to Captain Barrett who was walking about twenty five yards away. The Captain came running over and looked at the camp site. He determined that it had been used not too long ago by Indians. The remains of fish, rabbit and birds that had been eaten lay scattered near the site.

As they fanned out, other men found similar sites. They seemed to all be in a row. This confirmed the initial thinking that what the men had come across was the remains of camp sites used by the Indians to surround Fort Pitt.

Colonel Bouquet came forward to see what the scouts had found and then congratulated Gus on finding them. Gus replied, "I just found one sir. Mr. Andrews there found the other."

"Good job finding the first one, Gus. You have been quite a help to me on this march."

"Thank you, sir." replied Gus. He was a little embarrassed about the attention.

"Now Gus, go get that Indian of yours and see if he can tell us any more about this camp site and where his tribe might be now."

"Yes, sir." replied Gus and he ran off to where Newate was tied to the back of a supply wagon.

"Come on," said Gus, "it's time for you to be helpful."

He motioned for the Indian to come and they walked back up to the camp site.

Through the interpreter, Colonel Bouquet asked if Newate knew who had been at this encampment. He answered that he and his fellow Delaware warriors had camped there. Then the Colonel asked where the warriors would be now. Newate responded that he did not know. The Colonel did not believe him and once again drew his sword. Newate did not flinch, but finally said that perhaps they had gone home, many days walk from here. With no more questions for the Indian, he was escorted back to the wagon once again and tied there for the rest of the trip.

CHAPTER TWENTY-FOUR

Chief Natawatwees and Glikikan stayed off the roads the English used. They used the trails the Indians had been using for many years. The going was difficult for the son who had been shot in the leg, but it was even more difficult for the father and chief who had seen his middle son wounded and could not find his oldest or youngest sons. He held out little hope for his youngest son since it was his first battle and he had not been seen since the first encounter with the British when one of his braves said he saw him get shot. As they made their way along the trail, neither of the Indians had much to say. Natawatwees blamed himself for getting his tribe into this fight. Glikikan blamed himself for getting shot, only to anger his father and compel him to charge into the lines of the British.

As they made their way along, they heard the calls from other survivors. Little by little, the men from his village gathered around their chief. Neither of his sons was with them nor were many of his friends. The last charge into the lines that led to the flanking by the British killed many of his tribe. Some of these were men he had known all his life. Others were men the age of his sons with young families. Returning to the village having suffered such a defeat would be difficult, but his men were supportive and tried to show how the defeat was not his fault. Their words changed little about how he felt. He had lost. He had failed as a chief and a father. He was not sure how he was going to face his wife.

Natawatwees and his tribe gathered on the hill overlooking Fort Pitt. They knew they could not take the fort and the other tribes had scattered and were regrouping, presumably to make their own way home. They camped overnight at their original site they had used during the siege. In the morning they circled around to the north-west to find some of the canoes and rafts that had been used to bring the Wyandot and Shawnees across the Allegheny River to meet Colonel Bouquet. By mid-day, the tribe was across the river and back in their own territory. The fear of further confrontation was over and the men took their time searching for food before continuing their two day walk back to their village.

When the men neared the village, the dogs came out to meet them. There was great excitement as the women, children and old men came to meet the returning warriors. But it did not take long for the faces of the warriors to reveal what had happened. Natawatwees' wife came running to meet him and examined her son's leg. She looked quickly around for her other two boys and when she could not find them, she cried out in pain. She fell to the ground and sobbed for her sons. Chief Natawatwees tried to comfort her, but she would not be comforted by him. This was his fault; he let her baby boy go, and now he was gone forever. Soon Unamati came to her and together they cried for the boy who was at once a boy and a man, a son and potential husband. Words were not exchanged, but each knew what the other was feeling and their shared grief seemed to help.

CHAPTER TWENTY-FIVE

Colonel Bouquet remembered what had happened to Captain Grant when he and his men went marching into Fort Duquesne, but he felt that perhaps the sound of the pipes and drums would scare off any Indians that may be remaining. He knew that it would certainly inspire the troops who had been locked inside the fort since May. And so, just behind the scouts who once more fanned out in front of the army, marched the British 42nd regiment in their red coats and blue and green kilts. The "Black Watch" were a good fighting regiment who had distinguished themselves at Fort Ticonderoga, in the West Indies and most recently at Bushy Run. If there was to be any additional trouble, it would be good to have these men at the ready in the front of the lines. They were as proud of their piping as they were their fighting and so with all the gusto they could manage, the pipes and drums played a march that set the pace for the army to follow as it descended down the hill east of Fort Pitt and made its way to the point where the three rivers met.

The lookouts at Fort Pitt had reported seeing Indians making their way around the fort. They saw some on foot and some up river using canoes to cross the Allegheny. It seemed like this movement was not a strategy to reposition themselves, but one to remove themselves from the immediate area.

Captain Ecuyer was not sure what was happening and so he doubled the number of men watching from the lookout posts. He did not want to be caught unaware in the event the Indians decided to try to attack the fort again. His "gift" of diseased blankets did not seem to leave the Indians any less potent than they had been before. But what if they realized that he had given them something that was making them sick? Perhaps they were going to attack in revenge for his cruel treatment.

From the hill overlooking the point, Gus got his first look at Fort Pitt. It reminded him of a turtle with four legs sticking out and a head. The large earthen walls made it look pretty formidable. He could see why the Indians could not capture it. He scanned the area on his left and did not see any sign of Indians. What lie before him were rolling hills that steadily made their way down to the fort. He saw no Indians there either. Captain Barrett looked through his telescope at the fort and saw that the British flag was still flying. It was a sign that the fort had survived the siege. He announced what he saw and a cheer went out from the men nearby.

Gus was sent to get Colonel Bouquet and share the good news. He responded by nearly running into the Colonel as he was making his way to the front. Gus shared the good news and Colonel Bouquet also took a look at the fort he had helped build when he served under General Forbes.

"Alright men," the Colonel shouted, "look sharp and you pipers play those pipes like you've never played them before. Let them know we're coming, men!"

All the pipers and all the drummers marched together and the noise they made could have raised the dead. The army marched on steadily downward toward the fort.

Two of the lookouts were watching to the east to see if they could see any more activity from the Indians. No one had noticed any since the previous day. The tension was pretty high. Somehow, it was better to be able to look out and see them camped all around than to look out and see one here and there. What was happening did not make sense. One day the Indians were there, and the next they were gone. A few days later they were back in the area, but not at their previous posts. Everyone had some speculation as to what was going on and not knowing for sure seemed to make the situation worse.

As the men were watching, suddenly one of them saw a reflection of sunlight off to the east. As he squinted in that direction, he saw men coming, but was not able to make out who they were. The alarm was sounded and men ran to their posts to prepare for an attack. Captain Ecuyer came to the lookout that had seen the reflection and asked where the men were. He held up his telescope and began to focus on the area just as the whole fort heard the unmistakable sounds of bagpipes and drums.

"We're saved!" he shouted. "Thanks be to God. We're saved. Those crazy brothers must have gotten through."

All the men and women inside the fort jumped for joy and hugged each other in excitement. A Scottish regiment was on its way. The Indians had left the area. Life was much brighter that August morning for the people inside Fort Pitt.

After the initial celebration, Captain Ecuyer prepared his troops to receive the soldiers who were coming to his rescue. He was not sure who they were or who was in charge, but he was certainly happy to see and hear them coming.

As the troops got closer to the fort, it became obvious that there would be no surprise Indian attack. The scouts fell back and allowed the pipers and Colonel Bouquet to lead the way into the fort. Gus could see the large doors of the fort swing open and hear the cheers of the people inside as the army began to make its way past the gate into the parade ground. There were people lined up on both sides. The soldiers stood at attention and the civilians waved and shouted as the army made its way in.

Once inside, Captain Ecuyer, who was also a man from Switzerland, saluted Colonel Bouquet and extended his hand in welcome.

"Welcome, sir. We are most pleased that you have been able to come to our relief. I was not sure if the Watkins brothers had made it through or not."

"They did indeed, and in fact they have accompanied us back. They are brave young men and are to be commended for their work."

With that, the brothers came to the front where the officers stood and the soldiers and the civilians shouted, "Hip, hip, Hurrah! Hip, hip Hurrah!"

The flour was taken to storage and the women inside the fort began to make a meal in celebration of the British victory. Some of the men who had been cooped up in the fort went out in squads to fish along the banks of both the rivers. They caught bass, catfish and trout that was cooked and shared with everyone. Others went out to hunt to see if they could find rabbit or pheasant. Gus went with them and was able to kill a pheasant as it began to take flight from a field not far from the fort. It was a male ring-neck with those long brown tail feathers and that dark green head with a white ring around its neck. When they came back, they added their catch to the variety of foods being prepared for the feast. Everyone was joyful and excited to be freed from the siege. Those who were the heroes were also happy, for they had accomplished what they had set out to do.

After dinner, a few of the men played music and some people danced folk dances. The ladies who had been captives seemed to both enjoy the music and be saddened by it at the same time. Everyone was well behaved and even the scouts, who seemed to be the roughest men in the army, treated the ladies with respect. Some of them even asked a lady to dance. Gus saw a girl who was around ten watching the dancing and he asked her to be his partner. Her eyes lit up and she took his hand as they made their way in and out of squares. The evening did not end until the dancers and musicians were both worn out from the fun. What a relief it was to be free to live normal lives again.

One of the men who had been in the fort while it was under siege wrote a letter to his wife that evening. In it he said "You may be sure the sight of the troops was very agreeable to our poor garrison, being penned up in the fort from the 27th of May to the 9th of August, and the barrack rooms crammed with men, women and children, tho' providentially, no other disorder ensued than the small-pox."

CHAPTER TWENTY-SIX

The next morning as Gus was eating breakfast; Sergeant Caldwell said to him, "Do you see that Captain over there?" "Yes, replied Gus. "Who is he?"

"He is Captain William Trent from Virginia. He was responsible for building this fort in 1753. As you can see by the crowd around him, he is greatly respected by his fellow Virginians. They are happy to see that he is still well."

Sergeant Caldwell went over to Captain Trent and joined the crowd of Virginians who were taking a few minutes to catch up with each other. When the conversation had died down, he asked Captain Trent if he would mind giving him and Gus a tour of the fort. The Captain said he would be happy to and the three of them began to make their way around the fort. This fort, like the one at Bedford and the one at Ligonier was pentagonal shaped and seemed to fit well into the triangle formed by the two rivers as they joined to make the Ohio. They decided to begin by going to the south side of the fort that overlooked the Monongahela River. This side occupied the highest ground around the fort. As they looked out on the river, Gus noticed the steep bank on the opposite side. It seemed to rise up hundreds of feet. He commented that if the Indians had cannons up there, they could have easily fired down upon the fort. Trent agreed, but explained that the Indians had not seemed to be inclined to use cannon, but to hit and run instead. Then Captain Trent said, "On the other side of the fort there was an area that they had called Low Town, which had been a collection of helter-skelter cabins, shacks and storage buildings. All of those buildings were burned down at the beginning of Pontiac's uprising so that the Indians could not use the buildings to hide behind and attack the fort. It was a good thing too, because after they had us surrounded for several months, they shot at us for five days, but we did not sustain many casualties."

As they looked over the side of the fort, Captain Trent pointed out the continuous ditch that he called "The Isthmus". He explained, "That ditch there runs from the Monongahela across the land side of the fort there all the way over to the Allegheny. It joins up with the ditch that is dug around the whole fort to act like a moat. If you look over there where it runs, you'll see that the ditch is paralleled by the earthen embankment called an epaulement which is there to provide protection for an advance line of soldiers."

When they walked over to the east part of the fort, Captain Trent showed them the entrance road they had just come in and reminded them of the two draw bridges that crossed the isthmus. The triangular island between these two bridges served as added protection for the entrance and contained an underground guardhouse for prisoners.

Gus had forgotten about his Indian prisoner in all of the celebration, until they got here to the guardhouse where the prisoners were held. Some had been there since the siege began. Others had been taken after the battle. A few, like Gus' Indian, had been wounded and mercifully spared. It looked like the Indian's bandage had been changed again, and he seemed to be doing alright. Gus wondered what was going to become of him. He wished he could talk to him, speak his language without an interpreter. There were many questions he had for him.

As they left the guard house area, Captain Trent explained that unlike Ligonier, Fort Pitt was a dirt fort. It was simply a five sided parade ground that was bordered by five rows of buildings which were protected by five parallel mounds of earth shaped like arrow heads. Trent said, "These two sides toward the land that faces east, are supported by heavy walls faced with brick and stone. That revetment there is fifteen feet high. No Indian is going to get over or through it. Cannon balls will not even penetrate it. It encloses the music bastion and runs south there around the flag bastion."

Captain Trent then took Sergeant Caldwell and Gus down underneath the parade ground to storage areas that were five to seven feet below the ground surface. The first casement they came to was used to store powder for the cannon, the next was the artillery laboratory and the third was for supplies and provisions.

When they had seen many of the casements, Sergeant Caldwell said, "It looks like we got here just in time. Supplies look awfully low."

"Indeed they are," replied Captain Trent. "We have been rationing since the beginning of the siege. All the settlers and trappers came rushing into the fort and that made our situation even worse."

The tour moved onto the parade ground. Gus had seen the three barracks when they marched into the fort, but Captain Trent explained, "You see, we have three barracks here. They are all two stories high. That one over there behind the Low Town Curtain is the only one built of brick. It measures 190 by 20 feet in size. These three barracks can house about 1000 people." Gus noticed that there were three wells at the fort; unlike Fort Bedford where the soldiers had to pull water from the river. Captain Trent explained that they were fortunate to find good water running right under the fort. Captain Trent then pointed out a square log building for storage of flour that stood just as one entered the main gate. Gus had noticed it when they came into the fort. To the left Gus could see a frame officers' barracks. Behind the Monongahela Curtain was another frame officers' barracks. The Commandant's house was on the left. It was made of brick and had a cellar under it. Gus thought that it was the nicest building in the fort.

"Well, there you have it fellas," said Captain Trent. "She is a grand fort. The Indians were not able to overcome us in the siege and five days of attack. The worst thing that happened to us was the floods that damaged our walls the past two springs. But they were strong enough to save the parade ground and the casements from being flooded."

"It sure is a fine fort, Captain Trent," said Gus. "You must be very proud of it."

"I am. It has served us well. And I hope it will continue to do so."

"Thanks for the tour Captain Trent." said Sergeant Caldwell.

The men shook hands and the Captain went off to chat with some of the officers. Gus thought through the tour one more time in his head to memorize what was where. When he remembered the prison, he once again wondered what would become of the Indian he had shot.

CHAPTER TWENTY-SEVEN

Colonel Bouquet decided that his men needed to rest and take some time to heal themselves after their long march and battle. Although his goal was to punish those Indians involved in the uprising, he did not set out immediately to find them. He believed that he still had time before winter and that when the Indians returned home having suffered a defeat, they may be inclined to talk peace terms rather than fight again and lose more warriors.

And so the life at the fort returned to a more normal routine. When the men left the fort, they continued to go in larger numbers than normal, but they were able to hunt, fish and get fresh fruits that were abundant. Much of the meat was smoked and the fruits were dried for the winter season. Some of those who had come to the fort for protection slowly began to leave and resume their own lives again. The little village of Pittsboro outside the fort slowly began to fill up with inhabitants and visitors. The women captives began to become assimilated into life inside the fort and soon were helpful in many ways. Colonel Bouquet assured them all that just as soon as peace was made with the Indians and he could assure their safety, he would personally take them back east to their families.

Some of the vegetable gardens that had been planted in the spring were now full of ripe vegetables. Corn, beans, hay and oats were in need of attention. The soldiers pitched in and assisted the local folks as the harvest season approached.

The smokehouse at the fort was also a busy place. The men were on the river daily with nets, rods and spears catching fish they could smoke and cure. Gus enjoyed volunteering for this task and alternated between it and going out with the hunting parties to try to find deer, rabbit, pheasant, grouse, turkey or even squirrel that could be butchered and either used that night for dinner or dried for jerky.

As the hunters got to know each other, word got around that Gus was one of the best hunters in the fort. He had the ability to be patient. He knew nature and the animals in it. And, of course, he was a great shot.

One day, as the men were eating breakfast, one of the other scouts proposed a bet that by the end of the day he could bring back a bigger deer than Gus. People began to bet money on who would win this contest. The rules were soon established. The winner would be the one who brought back to the fort, before sunset that day, the deer that weighed the most after being gutted and field dressed. And the prize to the winner would be half of what was bet. The rest of the money would go to those who bet in his favor.

After getting permission from Captain Barrett, Gus and the other scout who proposed the bet set out to look for deer. Gus had been around the area a little over the past few weeks and had seen some signs of deer back east toward the mountains. One of the other men had gotten a deer not too far from the fort to the north. Gus decided to go east because he knew that area better. Beyond the hill where the Delaware had camped, the area was heavily wooded, but there were places with some open fields and streams as well with some swampy areas nearby. Gus remembered when he would go hunting with his father that the deer liked the trees for cover and food, especially acorns. They also liked pine trees to lie beneath and hide in. Deer ate flowering plants of all kinds, including weeds, honeysuckle and even small trees. So, Gus was on the lookout for an open field that led to dense shrubs and finally a thick forest. That kind of area would give him the best chance of seeing a deer. He planned to hide in the forest and shoot the deer as it came through the field or shrub.

Gus knew that the deer's sight was not as good as its hearing, so he made every effort to not make noise as he looked for the spot he wanted to use. He also knew that once he got himself established in a position where he could see the field in front of him, the other birds and animals would settle down and forest life would resume as if he were not even there. So, Gus intentionally moved slowly and walked along the ridgeline until he saw a spot that looked like it would be just right for his purpose.

After just a few more minutes walk, Gus had found a small apple tree that he climbed only high enough to be slightly off the ground to enable him to see any deer come by but not too high as to obstruct his view with branches and leaves.

Several hours went by before Gus even saw a deer. It was a doe that seemed pretty small. He felt sure that a bigger one or a buck would come by soon and decided to let that one walk by. After a little while a whole herd of doe came by. There were eight all together, but none of them looked much bigger than the first. They seemed like they were only about three feet tall. Gus decided once again to wait. He was determined to shoot a male deer that would be bigger and weigh more. His stomach told him that it was near dinner time before he saw another deer. This one was a buck. It was by itself as it made its way toward him just as the doe had earlier. Eventually, Gus could see that the deer was an eight point. He had a reddish brown coat that was typical for the summer season. His ears were big and moved from front to side in an attempt to pick up any warning of a problem. Gus decided that if he could get a clear shot, he would take it because this animal was pretty big. It had to be over three hundred pounds.

When the deer was about forty yards away, just as it was about to enter the shrubs, it stopped to eat some honeysuckle. Gus cocked his musket and took aim. He wanted to shoot the deer in the shoulder or midsection. He did not want to have to chase it after he shot it. He slowly squeezed the trigger, the gun fired, and the buck fell to the ground. He struggled to get back to his feet, but the musket ball had broken his left front shoulder and he could not get up. Gus reloaded the musket and fired once again. This time the deer was hit in the head and it was out of its misery. Gus quickly hurried down from his tree and made his way to the deer he had shot. He gutted it and cleaned it out quickly with his knife and hands. He wiped his hands on the grass and tied a short leather rope to the deer's antlers to enable him to pull it back to the fort.

As he made his way slowly back to the fort, Gus was thinking that he might have been better off looking for a deer closer by instead of a few miles away. But soon, he was back to the site where the Indians had camped. He decided to stop and rest a minute there before moving on. While there, Gus heard another musket fire not far away. He thought to himself that it must be the other scout who had bet with him. He became curious about how big a deer the other man had shot and so decided to make his way in that direction to see. Soon he came upon the other man field dressing a buck as well. But as he drew near, he heard the unmistakable cry of a mountain lion. So did the other scout. He put down his knife and began to look around for his musket. After he fired it at the deer, he had not reloaded it; he rapidly tried to reload the weapon with his bloody hands. In his haste, he dropped one ball and spilled some powder. Gus dropped his deer and continued to approach the area where he had first heard the mountain lion with his musket ready. Once again the lion cried. This time Gus thought that the sound came from behind the other man. His assumption was confirmed when the man spun around with his musket half loaded peering into the woods for the threat to his life. Within a second, Gus saw the big cat spring from an outcropping of rocks toward the scout. Gus took aim and fired as the animal was in mid-air. A cry let him know that he had hit the lion, but its force carried it onto the other scout and it knocked him to the ground. Before the lion could get up, Gus was on it with his knife. He sliced through the animal's neck and blood poured out onto the man beneath who had covered his head with his arms thinking that his life was surely over.

Gus rolled the mountain lion off the scout and asked him if he were alright. The man just lay there for a minute checking his arms, chest and face. There was blood everywhere. The lion's claws and teeth had made some impact, but after he wiped himself off, he realized that the greatest amount of blood had come from the lion. He would need some bandages, but would certainly live to see another day. As the scout looked around and began to take stock of his situation he could not believe his good fortune. Not only had Gus saved his life, but from the looks of it, Gus had not yet shot a deer and he may also win the bet. The man said to Gus, "Why don't you just clean that lion you shot and take it back to the fort?"

Gus replied, "I can't because I have that big buck lying over there to continue to drag back."

The man walked over to where Gus had dropped his deer and could see that his own deer was not as big.

"Well," said the man, "I guess I owe you both my thanks and congratulations. You have saved my life and won the bet. Nice going Gus."

The two scouts shook hands and finished cleaning the deer. Then they both began to make their way back to the fort. The older man had a deeper appreciation for the younger and vowed as they walked along dragging their deer, that he would never bet against him again.

When the two scouts got back to the fort, the sentries saw them coming, and spread the word that the men were coming in together, each dragging a deer. A few of the scouts went out to meet them and to help them bring in the deer. Both of the deer were hung up by their antlers and tied to the end of a board that had been placed over a tree limb. After a few seconds, Gus' deer began to tilt the board downward indicating to all that it was heavier than the other deer. Gus was declared the winner of the contest and given the prize money. Everyone cheered for Gus. He was quickly becoming one of the more popular scouts in the fort.

As the cheers died down, the older scout told the story of the mountain lion and how Gus had shot it in mid-air and then finished it off with his knife. Once again cheers went up for Gus. The men came over one by one and patted him on the back and shook his hand. It was one thing to be a good shot. But it was something else all together to save another man's life. Today he had done both.

CHAPTER TWENTY-EIGHT

One day, Gus decided that he wanted to learn a little of the language the Indians used. He asked the man who had been the interpreter to teach him a few things. Since life at the fort was slow now while the wounded men were recovering, the man agreed. Gus learned simple phrases like greetings and some basic questions. Then he began to walk around the fort asking the interpreter to name items that he saw. Day after day they would make their rounds together and soon Gus had learned the Indian names for many items in the fort.

Gus asked the interpreter to go out in the woods to name trees, streams, flowers and animals. And once again, he learned these items. Soon, he was conversing with the interpreter using only the language of the Delaware. As the weeks went by he learned enough to keep up pretty well. There were still words that he did not know the Indian name for, but he was learning more and more every day.

Several of the other scouts had noticed Gus and the interpreter exchanging words in another language and asked what they were doing. Gus explained that he wanted to learn the language of the Indians. One scout replied while holding up his musket, "This is the only language they understand. And besides, as soon as settlers start coming over those mountains, those Indians will have to learn the King's English."

Gus wondered if he had been wasting his time, but decided that the other man was wrong. His family had come to America, but they spoke both German and English. He decided that it would not hurt to understand the language of the Indians, and so he kept working on his vocabulary with the interpreter as often as he had a chance.

One day Gus went to the prison cell to check on the Indian he had shot. He was pleased to see that the bandage was gone and the shoulder was healing. It was still red and looked tender, but the hole had healed over. Gus began to feel better knowing that the Indian would recover fully. While there, Gus decided to have a seat against a wall and listen to the Indians talk to one another. They did so freely because they did not know that Gus had been learning their language.

In their own tongue, one of the Indians asked the one Gus had shot, "Do you think your father will try to surround the fort again and starve out these soldiers?"

"I do not know," replied Newate. "Many of our warriors were killed in the battle. There may not be enough to do it again."

A third chimed in, "Chief Natawatwees will never give up, especially if he knows his son is rotting away in this prison."

Many of the others agreed, but Newate said, "I'm not so sure that he knows I'm here."

The others fell silent. There hopes for a rescue had just grown dimmer.

Gus slowly got up from his place against the wall and casually made his way out of the prison. Then he ran about the fort until he found the interpreter and asked him what a word meant. The Interpreter said it was the word for Chief. Then he asked him how he knew the word and Gus explained what he had just heard. The interpreter smiled a broad smile and said, "Well done, Gus. Well done indeed. Come on, we need to tell the Colonel."

Colonel Bouquet was sitting behind a desk in a small office writing a correspondence to Major-General Amherst when Gus and the interpreter were shown in.

Colonel Bouquet said, "Well, if it isn't the best shot at the fort and the best interpreter with him. Gentlemen, how can I help you?"

The interpreter looked at Gus and Gus looked at him. Finally Colonel Bouquet said, "Gus you start, whatever it is, it can't be all that bad."

Gus began by telling him, "Well sir, I've been learning the Indian language from the interpreter here. And just now I was over at the prison and overheard a conversation between the Indian I shot and two others. It seems that the others were hoping that the Indians would come back to rescue them, especially since the one I shot was Chief Natawatwees' son."

Colonel Bouquet looked at the interpreter as if to have him confirm what had just been said. The interpreter simply nodded.

"Good God. We have Chief Natawatwees' son in our prison? He is the one you shot and tied up? Good God in heaven. What a bargaining chip we have gentlemen. What a bargaining chip we have indeed"

"But the Chief's son said he did not know if his father even knew he was alive," said Gus.

"Did you shoot him on the first day at Edge hill?" asked the Colonel.

"Yes," replied Gus, "just as the fighting was getting started."

"That means that he did not return to his people that night." said Colonel Bouquet.

"His father broke off the fighting and ran home. He must have thought that his son was dead. Gentlemen, we have ourselves an advantage now as we try to get these Indians to agree to peace talks. Your Indian may come in very handy indeed, Gus."

Colonel Bouquet slapped Gus on the shoulder and offered him his hand in congratulations. "Well done, young man. Well done. As of today, you will get an increase in pay grade. You have shown initiative, Gus. By God, well done! Now sit over there men, while I call my officers together to discuss how we might proceed from here."

Within a few minutes, the small room was packed full of men. They all gave Gus and the interpreter a sideways glance as if to ask what they had done, but the look on the Colonel's face was not stern at all. In fact, he seemed elated.

"Gentlemen," began Colonel Bouquet, "I'm sure you all know by now young Gus, the scout. He has lately been learning to speak the language of the Delaware Indians from our interpreter."

The officers were impressed and Captain Barrett winked his approval.

"Let me tell you what information Gus has learned as a result of his new skills. The Indian he shot back at Edge Hill, is none other than the son of the Delaware Chief." He paused for a moment to let this information sink in. Then he said, "What I would like from you is some suggestions on how best to use this Indian to get the peace we are seeking."

"Why not offer him in exchange for any captives they may have?" suggested one officer.

"How about holding onto him to see if his father will bargain first and then handing him over?" suggested another.

"We could take the lad to their village when we go and if the negotiations don't go well, we could then use him to get the peace we seek," suggested one of the officers from the Black Guard.

"That's it," Colonel Bouquet declared. "That's exactly how we will do it. In the mean time, Gus, could you stop by the prison more often to listen in on more conversation?"

"Certainly, sir." replied Gus. Then he and the interpreter stood, saluted and left the room.

Gus was so excited that he had been able to help. At the same time he was still amazed that he had shot the Chief's son. Maybe this is the reason he had spared his life. Maybe by using the Indian in the bargaining, no more lives will be lost. That would be good.

CHAPTER TWENTY-NINE

G us made it a point to be around the prison area every day. He would look at the men there, but pretend to not pay any attention to what they were saying. In this manner he was able to pick up bits and pieces of information about each of the men and what they longed for if they were ever released.

One day the men were obviously teasing the Indian he had shot about a girl back in the village. One of the men said something like, "You can run like a deer, but you'll never get away from her." Gus imagined from these comments that the girl in the village was the one pursuing the Indian he had shot and that he was not married, but single like himself. This made him think about Elizabeth and the promise he had made to himself to win her hand. So far, he had a job in the army with one raise given after just a few months. He had fought well and brought Colonel Bouquet to the sight of the skirmish at Edge Hill. And he had shot the chief's son and saved another man's life. If that did not impress Rev. McGregor, he would just have to try harder. But one day Elizabeth would be his wife. He decided to write his uncle a letter and in it he put another one for Elizabeth that he asked him to give to her. He felt bad about going behind Rev. McGregor's back, but he did not want her father to intercept the letter.

The letter said:

"Dear Elizabeth,

I miss you very much. I hope you are well. I am fine. We have reached Fort Pitt safely after a fierce battle near the

Bushy Run outpost. I was shot in the arm, but it was only a flesh wound. It has nearly healed by now.

After the battle, some of the men from Virginia rescued women and girls who were captives. We have them with us at the fort. Colonel Bouquet said that he would bring them back east once we have established peace in this region. They have been through a lot. I feel sorry for them. Some of them saw their husbands and fathers killed. They all seem to be happy to be with us now.

During the battle, I shot an Indian in the shoulder after he narrowly missed shooting me in the head. He is nearly healed now too. But I found out that he is the son of the Chief of the Delaware Indians.

I've been learning their language. It has been interesting. I learned that he has a girl in his village that likes him. When I heard that, it made me think of you.

I hope to be home before winter. Please take care of yourself.

Yours truly,
Gus"

After it was sent off with the other mail going east, Gus wondered if he had done the right thing. He followed the longings of his heart, but it was not very honorable. He was a little troubled by it.

When he returned to the prison to listen to the conversations the next day, the Indian who had been shot was telling one of the others that when he had gone back to the village after killing the English trapper, he was aroused when Unamati had given him a hug. At that moment he realized that he saw her as more than a friend. He wanted to take her to be his wife. But now here he was and he did not know when or if he would ever see her again. He was sure that his father assumed he was dead or he would have tried a prisoner exchange. They had many white prisoners in the village. Maybe Unamati would find another man since he had not come home.

The other Indian listened to his concerns and tried to reassure him, but his words had little effect on Newate.

Gus reported what he had heard to Colonel Bouquet. The Colonel was once again grateful for now he had a way to entice the young Indian into talking to him and cooperating.

Gus and the interpreter were sent to the prison to get Newate. The guards ushered him back to Colonel Bouquet's office and stood guard over him.

Colonel Bouquet asked him, "Where does your tribe live?"

The Interpreter repeated the question. The Indian was a little hesitant and then replied,

"To the west, on the Sandusky River."

Colonel Bouquet asked, "Do you have a family?"

Newate replied, "I have no woman yet."

Then Colonel Bouquet asked, "Are you in love with a girl from your village?"

Newate looked surprised that he would know this and began to answer no, but then said, "Yes, I love a girl named Unamati."

When he said it he stood up a little straighter as if he were proud to have made that statement.

"Newate," continued Colonel Bouquet, "If you promise to lead us to your village in an effort to make peace, I will promise that you will see Unamati within two months."

Newate's eyes widened in disbelief.

"What will you ask for in your peace talks?" he asked. "Will my people be forced to move? Will you take their land as the English have done before?"

"No", replied the Colonel. "All I want is your father's word that he will stop raiding the settlers and the release of all of the captives."

Again Newate looked shocked. "How do you know my father?" he asked.

The Colonel replied that it was his job to know these things and once again pressed for an agreement.

Finally Newate agreed that he would take them to his village.

The Colonel thanked him and the soldiers began to lead him away. But Newate paused and asked another question. He asked the interpreter the name of the boy who had shot him. After the interpreter told the Colonel what he had asked, the Colonel introduced him to Gus.

He said, "Gus here is the best shot in the fort, and the best hunter as well. Since he shot you in the shoulder, I'd say that that is where he was aiming. You can thank him for sparing your life."

Newate looked hard at Gus and then said to the Interpreter "Give the good hunter my thanks." Then he put his right hand out and as Gus put his out, the Indian grasped it not by the hand but up higher on the arm, just below the elbow. The two enemies stood there at the beginning of a new truce, if only between one young scout and one young brave.

The guards took Newate back and Colonel Bouquet was once again pleased with how things had turned out. "I believe we have the makings of peace, gentlemen," he said to Gus and the interpreter. "Yes, indeed, I believe we do."

CHAPTER THIRTY

As the harvest season ended and the men began to heal from their wounds, Colonel Bouquet brought in reinforcements from the east. More men, ammunition and supplies were a sure sign that the army would be moving out soon to finish the job of stopping the raids and establishing peace.

Colonel Bouquet asked Captain Barrett to have his scouts begin to probe westward along the Ohio for the Indian villages he wanted to visit. The missions were to be undertaken very carefully. That meant the men would have to cross the Allegheny and then walk westward until they located the villages they were looking for. Although they had a general idea of where they were along the Ohio, they had not been there and did not want to be surprised.

The first village they came to was occupied by the Shawnee and Mingo Indians. It was just down river from Pittsboro. The Indians called this place Sewickley. As the scouts saw signs of life and activity, they slowly made their way forward and watched. Captain Barrett gave them assignments. Some of the men counted how many braves were in the village. Others tried to determine the total number of people living there. Gus and his group tried to see if there were any white captives in this village. The rest of the men spread out to make sure they were not detected. A small scouting party could soon find themselves as captives if they were discovered.

After about half an hour, the men withdrew from their positions and reported what they had seen. The two most significant numbers were the number of warriors and the number of captives. The men could not agree, but determined that they saw at least twenty captives, both men and women. This information was noted by Captain Barrett and the men crept through the woods to sneak around the village so that they could proceed along the path that they hoped would lead them to the next village.

The men decided to stay near the Ohio, thinking that most of the villages would be found there. The river flowed northwest from Pittsboro. Several days after leaving Sewickley, they found a tributary the Indians referred to as the Beaver River. As they camped there, they could see evidence of the beavers living and building along the river. It would be a good place to trap if one were a trapper. But these men had no time for that. They avoided camp fires and lived on dried fruit, meat and whatever they could find as they made their way through the forest. There was still some fruit available on the apple trees and berry bushes. Nuts were also available at this time of the year, so the men ate whatever they could find to supplement what they carried with them.

The men were far away from the fort now and tried to avoid detection at all costs. They never walked through open fields or meadows. If they had to cross a river that emptied into the Ohio, they did so one at a time and slipped from shore to shore as quickly as possible. Fortunately, it was fall and most of the rivers and tributaries were shallow.

By following one of the tributaries, the Muskingum, north, inland a little ways, they came upon a village. They divided the responsibilities and went to work observing. Once again, white captives were found in this village.

On up the Muskingum they went until they found a village at Coshocton. There seemed to be mostly Shawnee and Seneca at this village. Very few captives were noted. Captain Barrett decided to return to the Fort after this observation because their supplies were running out and he had seen enough to give Colonel Bouquet knowledge of where some of the villages were located. With a little luck, Gus' Indian and the other captives at the fort would provide additional information.

The men were a little more relaxed as they made their return trip to Pittsboro. They may also have been motivated by hunger pangs, but whatever the reason was, they made good time back into Pennsylvania. As they passed the Beaver River once again, the Ohio River ran through a valley with hills on both sides. While making their way along a well worn path, the lead scout suddenly stopped and raised his hand. Not all of the men were paying attention and several of them ran into the men who had stopped in front of them. The sounds of grumbling and muskets clanking against each other let the approaching Indian hunting party know that someone was in the woods making their way toward them. It seemed like both sides just stood there for a minute until Captain Barrett gave the signal for the men to spread out into the surrounding forest. This they did with both speed and stealth. Unlike the militia or the British soldiers, these men were dressed to blend in to the surroundings and they knew the woods. Each man quickly found a tree or a bush to hide behind.

The Indians were a hunting party of Shawnee from the village at Sewickley. They had been hunting in the area and were now on their way back home carrying three deer with them. When the party of ten men heard the noise on the path up ahead, they stopped and listened. There was some other noise, but they could not be sure what or who made the sound. They decided to lay the deer down and investigate. Very slowly the Indians continued on the path. Some carried muskets and others carried bows and arrows that they had drawn, ready to shoot. As they made their way along the path, the Indians looked on both sides as well as ahead. When they got to the place where the scouts were hiding, one of the Indians pointed to some marks on the path. He motioned to the others to look as well. What they saw were shoe prints left behind by Gus and the scouts. The Indians began to look more closely into the woods around them to try to determine if anyone was still there.

Though there were more scouts than Indians, Captain Barrett did not want a fight at this place. He was not sure if there were more Indians around to hear musket fire, so, he waited.

The Indians looked and walked slowly up the path and back down again. Then they went back to where they left their deer and came back up the path again. They passed the spot where the scouts were hiding and continued on the trail.

After the Indians passed by, Captain Barrett came out from behind his tree and signaled for the others to do the same. When they were all back on the path and heading away from the Indians, Gus noticed a sound and then some movement off to his left. He realized in an instant that the Indians had begun to double back to try to surround the scouts. He called out a warning to Captain Barrett who once more told the men to get into the woods. Now they had some protection, but it was every man for himself. It appeared as though there was going to be a fight whether he liked it or not. It did not take long before the arrows began to fly. And once that happened, the muskets began to return fire.

Gus found himself standing behind a tree that offered him some cover and he watched the area where he had first noticed movement. An Indian must surely be around there somewhere. Soon, he noticed a branch move in a tree. Then he saw an Indian pulling back the string on his bow. Gus lifted his musket and fired. The Indian fell to the ground and did not get up. Gus knelt down to take advantage of the bushes for more cover and reloaded his musket. He stood up and watched for signs of movement. Captain Barrett was about twenty yards away also preparing to fire when an arrow struck him in the left arm. He dropped his musket and tried to pull the arrow out so he could tie a cloth around the wound. Gus looked back in the direction the arrow had come from and saw the Indian who had seen his first arrow find his enemy preparing to shoot again. Gus took aim and fired. The second Indian fell to the ground. This one had a hole right in the middle of his chest. He would not get up either. Gus ran to Captain Barrett's side and helped him take out the arrow. He tied a strip of cloth that he tore from the bottom of his shirt around the Captain's arm and propped him up against the tree, handing him his musket. Then he reloaded his own musket and stood guard over his wounded leader. Gus was looking straight ahead and did not notice the Indian who was creeping up behind him. The Indian moved slowly trying to get a clear shot. On his final step, he broke a branch and Gus dove to the ground just as the musket ball passed through the air where he had been. The Indian charged forward with his tomahawk raised. The war cry he made was enough to scare most men, but Gus had heard them before, and this was just one more Indian. The man got to within ten feet before Gus could roll over and aim. The ball hit the side of the Indians' head but did not kill him. He landed on his stomach and did not get up right away. The bullet must have dazed him a bit. This gave Gus the opportunity to pull out his own tomahawk and smash the Indian over the head. The opening in the Indian's head spouted blood on Gus' pants and hands. He just stood over the dead man and watched as the blood flowed out onto the ground.

Gus' trance was broken when he heard Captain Barrett call him to help him up. Gus shook himself a bit, wiped his hands on his pants and offered the Captain his hand to pull him up.

"My God, Gus", shouted the Captain, "I'm glad you're on my side."

"Thanks," replied Gus.

"Now, reload in case we are not done with this bunch."

"Yes, sir", replied Gus and he went about his task as quickly as possible. Then he went and gathered up the Indian's gun and took his ammunition.

In a few minutes, the fighting was over. The scouts began to count the dead. Four of their own were killed and two injured, including the Captain. All ten of the Indians were killed. Gus had killed three by himself.

Some of the scouts began to take scalps, but Captain Barrett stopped them and told them to quickly find places to hide the bodies so they could not be seen from the path. Then he had his men pick up the three deer and carry them back to the fort. Another piece of cloth was found to make a sling for his arm and one of the men carried his musket. He explained that he wanted them to hurry on their way back to the fort and so the men took turns helping him and the other wounded scout. They also took turns carrying the deer.

The going was slow, but they managed to get away from the spot where the fighting had occurred without any further incident. They camped overnight and at first light snuck by the village at Sewickley and were soon paddling their way across the Allegheny to Pittsboro and Fort Pitt.

The sentries announced their return and it did not take long for people to turn out to see the scouts bring back the wounded men and three deer.

Colonel Bouquet saw the Captain's arm and asked for an explanation.

"Well," replied Captain Barrett, "we were about a day's walk away when we came across a hunting party. We hid and let them pass, but they doubled back and attacked us. We lost four men and two of us were wounded. But we killed ten Indians and took their deer."

"You can tell me more about this after you get that arm treated. Now you and the other scout who was wounded, go get some medical attention. Please tell the rest of your men, 'Well done!'"

"Yes, sir." replied Captain Barrett. "But before I go, I should tell you that Gus Giron was the one who saw the Indians sneak around us to attack us. If not for his warning, we may have lost more men. He is also personally responsible for killing three of the ten Indians and saving my life."

"Well," said Colonel Bouquet, "Gus has turned out to be quite the scout. We'll have to find another way to reward him for his good service."

While Captain Barrett made his way to receive medical treatment, Gus and the others took the deer to the kitchen to be butchered for a much needed meal. After he had eaten some of the venison, beans and carrots, Gus went off to the trading store to sell the musket he had taken from the Indian he killed. He then sent the money home to his uncle along with a long letter telling him of his travels into Ohio and the Indian attack.

When nightfall came, Gus found a place to lie down and fell immediately to sleep. The letter home had made him think of Elizabeth and this night she was in his dreams.

CHAPTER THIRTY-ONE

On October 1st, sentries announced the arrival of several Indians. When they were escorted into the fort, the interpreter told Colonel Bouquet that they came to warn him not to try to enter their villages. They told him that he should leave the area because his army was so small and the soldiers were outnumbered, but Colonel Bouquet did not believe them. He sent them away. Two days later two chief's came to the Fort to talk with Colonel Bouquet. They told him that they had signed a treaty with Lieutenant Bradstreet, but once again Bouquet took a strong stance saying that he had heard about this treaty, but that they had not kept it. They had killed a man near Bedford, as well as a few in Virginia and another from the fort whose head had been cut off and stuck up on a pole near the path. He explained that he did not believe these to be the actions of Indians at peace. He told them they had not kept their word and that his army would soon be coming to establish peace.

After much deliberation, Colonel Bouquet finally consented to give the Indians one more chance. He told the chiefs, "Go home to your villages and tell all of the tribes near you that what I demand for peace is the surrender all of your captives. If you do not agree to live in peace and return all of your captives, you and all your people will be killed."

The next day several chiefs from the Shawnee and Delaware tribes returned to promise that they would obey his commands. Bouquet was pleased with their quick response, but warned them that if the demands were not met, his army would destroy their entire tribe.

Over the past few months, while his men were resting and recuperating, Colonel Bouquet's original army had been supplemented by additional militia until nearly one thousand; five hundred men were now ready to establish peace in the Ohio Territory. Many of these additional men were frontiersmen who were willing to volunteer to serve on this expedition to either make peace with the Indians or to crush them in their villages. Colonel Bouquet left Fort Pitt on October 3rd and began to visit the villages that Captain Barrett and the scouts had seen. Since Captain Barrett was still recovering from his wound, Colonel Bouquet asked Gus to lead the way. He then instructed Gus to get the Indian he had shot to take with them. They might need him to lead the way to his village. They visited the Shawnee at Sewickley first and talked with Chief Keissenautcha. He promised that his tribe would be at peace and handed over white men, women and children captives as required by Colonel Bouquet. Then the men marched on, following the Ohio as they had done before. On October 13th, Colonel Bouquet and his army reached the forks of the Muskingum and Tuscarawas Rivers. By the 16th of October, Bouquet met with Chief Kiyaschuta, a chief of the Senecas, as well as Chiefs Custaloga and Castor of the Delaware. The Delaware chiefs gave Bouquet eighteen white captives. They tried to blame all of the troubles between the Indians and the British on the young braves, but Bouquet would not accept that explanation. He continued to meet with the tribes one by one and continued to press his threat of total destruction if white captives were not returned. He claimed that he would do all he could to restrain his men and the white people in the East who wanted revenge as long as the Indians returned all the captives, including the English, French and former slaves within twelve days. They were told to provide these captives with enough food, clothing and horses to make the trip to Fort Pitt. The Indians agreed to everything Bouquet had demanded, but he did not trust them, so he moved his army up the Muskingum River to Coshocton. He and his army were right in the middle of Indian country where he could strike out at any tribe who did not follow through on his demands. Over the next several days, the Indians brought or sent in their captives.

Chief Natawatwees had been invited to attend a peace conference by Bouquet, but he did not attend. His grief over the loss of two sons and many men prevented him from ever wanting to see another white man. He certainly did not want to be at peace with them. He chose to simply ignore them as much as possible. Eventually, Colonel Bouquet and Lieutenant Bradstreet, who had been dealing with the Indians along the great lake region, joined forces. The Colonel asked Gus to bring the Indian he had shot to his tent. There, the Colonel reminded him of the bargain they had made at Fort Pitt and told him to lead the army to his village. This he did, with some obvious concerns that Colonel Bouquet would honor his part of the bargain and not wipe out his entire village.

As the combined army approached Natawatwees' settlement, Colonel Bouquet ordered the scouts ahead to see what they were up against. Gus and the others once again counted men and captives and returned to the Colonel with the information. Colonel Bouquet then gave the order for his men to surround the village and to slowly make their way toward it so that the Indians would see that they were surrounded. A dog was the first to notice something wrong and it began to bark at the strange men who were approaching the village. Soon the villagers saw the soldiers and the word was spread quickly. Natawatwees attempted to escape, but was captured by several of the Highlanders and brought back to the center of the village.

Some of the men recognized him from the battle at Bushy Run. He had fought bravely, but had made a mistake when he rushed too quickly into the lines that he thought were collapsing.

Colonel Bouquet had the interpreter come forward and through him asked, "Were you at the battle near Bushy Run outpost?"

"Yes," replied Natawatwees, "I was there and I lost many braves and two sons in that battle. You are a brave soldier, Colonel Bouquet, unlike many other white men."

Colonel Bouquet replied, "Thank you Chief Natawatwees. You too are quite brave. I am sorry to hear that you lost a son at the battle. I have come today to make peace with you and your people. All you have to do is return your white captives and promise me that you and your braves will no longer attack the white settlers."

The chief saw no need for more killing and could see that he was in no position to disagree, yet he hesitated to sign the agreement.

"Now," said Colonel Bouquet, "you say you lost two sons in the battle at Bushy Run. Is one of them named Newate?"

The question shook Natawatwees to the bone.

"How do you know this?" he demanded.

Colonel Bouquet called for Gus to untie Newate and bring him up to the meeting. When the father and son saw each other, they ran to greet each other with arms wide open. They laughed and cried and smiled.

"You're alive! You're alive! I thought you were dead. They told me you were killed."

"I was shot in the shoulder," replied Newate, "but the man who shot men tied me up and treated my wound. He saved my life." "Where is this man?" asked Chief Natawatwees. "He is the one who untied me just now. They call him Gus." The chief called Gus to his side. Colonel Bouquet nodded his approval. The Chief said, "Thank you for taking care of my son and bringing him home to me safely." The interpreter was beginning to interpret when Gus replied, "You are welcome."

The Chief was surprised to hear Gus respond in his own tongue and Newate was amazed. Then he understood how the Colonel had known about Unamati. He had been tricked and now he realized it. He smiled at Gus and Gus smiled back. They both looked at Colonel Bouquet and he too had a smirk on his face. "We will agree to your peace terms Colonel Bouquet," Chief Natawatwees said. "We will smoke the peace pipe. But first, let me take my son to see his mother."

Chief Natawatwees and Newate were given permission to go to their longhouse where Gus' mother was waiting, not knowing for sure what the soldiers were going to do. The village was surrounded and Natawatwees had told her to stay inside with the other women of the family. Two soldiers were asked to escort them to their longhouse, but as they began to go, Natawatwees stopped and asked Gus to go with them. Once more, Colonel Bouquet nodded his approval.

When Natawatwees entered the longhouse, he called to his wife. When she came to his side, he called his son into the home. Once more the tears began to flow. This time a mother, a son, a father and many other family members celebrated the return of one they believed to be dead. After the hugs and tears, Newate's mother asked him what had happened and how he got home. At that point, Chief Natawatwees called for Gus to come in. Soon, between Gus and Newate, the story was retold. Newate told them how he shot at Gus, who happened to bend down just as he fired, and Gus told how he waited to see the rifle stick out from behind the tree once again before he fired. That explained the shoulder wound. They both told the rest of the story from their own perspective. Newate told about Gus' scouting and shooting ability. Gus was a little embarrassed about all of the attention, but thought it may be a way for Newate to explain why he was shot in the first place. Newate's mother thanked Gus for taking care of her son and saving his life when he could have easily let him die of his wound. It seemed odd to Gus that he was being thanked, none-the-less, he accepted. The battle seemed so far behind him now. But now was the time to make amends and move on. It occurred to Gus that this family felt the same way.

After a few minutes of questions for both Gus and Newate, his mother called for one of the young women who lived there and sent her out of the longhouse to bring someone back. Gus did not hear clearly who she was told to retrieve, but the look on Newate's face made him realize that it must be the girl he liked and who liked him. When Newate looked his way, Gus winked. Newate did not know how to respond, so he just gave Gus a gentle shove. This brought out a chuckle from Gus and laughter from the whole family. It was nearly impossible to think that these two enemies, as of a few months ago, were now beginning to act more like brothers.

Chief Natawatwees said to Gus, "We owe you a debt that we can never repay. You have brought back to life one that was dead to us. What can I give you in return for my son?"

Gus replied, "I did not spare his life to simply return him to you. You make me out to be better than I am. I was hoping that by saving his life, he would be able to help us in some way."

"Was he?" asked the Chief.

"Not willingly," answered Gus. "I learned to speak your language from the interpreter and just listened in on the conversations of the Indian captives. I learned about a girl that likes Newate and Colonel Bouquet told Newate he would never see you or her again unless he led us to your village."

"You bribed him?" asked Chief Natawatwees.

"Yes," replied Gus, "and he lived up to his end of the bargain only after repeated reassurance that no harm would fall upon this village. Colonel Bouquet agreed that none here would be hurt so long as you agreed to sign the new peace agreement."

"It seems as if my son has learned a few lessons about negotiation and the need for peace," replied the Chief, "but, I was not aware that Newate had a favorite girl in the village. Why is it that the father is always the last to know these things?"

Just at that moment, Unamati came running through the open door. She slowed down only long enough to give the chief a brief greeting and then ran to Newate and gave him a long hug that embarrassed everyone. And for the third time, tears of joy flowed.

Finally, the Chief declared, "Today we will make peace with the white men again. Prepare a feast for our people and the soldiers and we will eat and smoke the pipe together. The British and the long knives will be our friends."

Everyone cheered and the women hurried around to spread the word. The Chief came out of the longhouse and asked Colonel Bouquet if he could send out some hunting parties to bring back some game for the feast. The Colonel agreed and preparations were under way. Newate asked his father if he could go along and Natawatwees replied "Yes, so long as Gus goes with you." This brought laughter from the Indians and, once interpreted, laughter from the soldiers as well.

Within a few hours, the men had brought back a large assortment of game to eat. Deer, rabbit, pheasant and fish were cooked along with corn, sweet potatoes and beans. By evening all was prepared and the meal was served. Gus and Colonel Bouquet were given places of honor with the chief and his family. Gus was seated next to Newate with Unamati sitting on the other side of her man. Now that he was back, he was not going to get away. She made up her mind to encourage Newate to talk to her father so that they could be married.

After the meal, Chief Natawatwees told everyone that he would agree to the terms of peace that Colonel Bouquet brought to him. There would be no more war with the white men and he would return all of the white captives in the village to the fort. Then he thanked Colonel Bouquet and Gus for bringing his son home. He presented Gus with deerskin leggings, an embroidered shirt and moccasins to show his gratitude. Gus accepted them graciously and tried them on to see if they fit. Newate's mother was pleased that they fit and smiled at the sight of a white boy dressed in clothes she had made for her son.

CHAPTER THIRTY-TWO

The Indians were true to their word. On the 9th of November, Indians brought thirty-two Virginia men, fifty- eight Virginia women and children, forty-nine Pennsylvania men, and sixty-seven Pennsylvania women and children to Fort Pitt. Those from tribes living farther away took a little longer to get to the fort, but Colonel Bouquet could see that the Indians were earnest. A squad from the fort made their way to report this news to Bouquet. He was pleased. It was time to move his army back to the fort. He had accomplished his mission. In a month and a half, by a show of force and by hard-headed bargaining, the redoubtable Swiss soldier had finally reaped the results of his victory at Bushy Run. In this campaign without a battle, he gained more fame than in all his previous campaigns and so captured the attention of his superior in the British Command.

Colonel Bouquet decided to return to the fort on November 18th. By this time the summer had turned to fall and the men were happy to be going back to the shelter and warmth of the fort. The soldiers began their return trip with less anxiety and a great deal of pride in their accomplishment. Gus and the other scouts were leading the way. He was wearing his new clothes. The mood of the army was very upbeat. The men were pleased that there was no additional fighting and looked forward to living in peace with the Indians once again. The Highlanders played their pipes and drums as they marched and life was enjoyable, somehow, for the first time in many months. It took them only ten days to get back to Pittsboro.

By the time Colonel Bouquet and his army got back, there were more than two hundred captives waiting for him at the fort.

Some of the children had grown up with the Indians and were not comfortable with the white people. Others were happy to be freed and celebrated with songs and hymns and prayers. Still others were a bit reserved and tried to keep their emotions under control until they could sort things out. One of the men who had volunteered to help in the campaign was looking at the group of released prisoners and saw his brother whom he thought was dead. He called him by name and ran to him, dropping him musket and hugging him while tears rolled down his face.

"O, praise God!" he said. "O, thank God!"

The men began to slap each other on the back and look at each other closely. Tears continued to roll out of the eyes of both men and soon, others were crying for joy that these two had been reunited.

A man from Virginia recognized his former neighbor. She had been taken a year earlier. Her hair was longer and she wore Indian style clothes, but he recognized her. She looked sad and displayed little emotion. The Virginian remembered that her husband and grown boys had been killed and she had been taken. He called out to her, but she just stared. Finally, he went over to her and gently touched her on the arm and said "Mary, Mary Hilton, is that you?"

She looked at him and said nothing for a long time. Finally, she asked, "Are they all dead?"

"Yes. We buried them next to the church. I made the markers myself."

Then she cried softly as she laid her head on the shoulder of her former neighbor and grieved for her loved ones.

Gus watched scene after scene similar to this where people connected with one another. There were tears of sadness and tears of joy. He tried to imagine what those who had been prisoners must be feeling, seeing friends and family. He was glad for them; happy that he had something to do with their reunion. But he also was sad for those who did not have anyone who knew them. There were many who were in this last category.

Once the Indians had fulfilled their part of the bargain, the chiefs came to Fort Pitt and presented Bouquet with a wampum belt as a sign of peace. One of the chiefs declared, "With this belt we assemble and bury the bones of those who have been killed in this unhappy war, which the evil spirit excited us to kindle." Bouquet accepted the belt and then surprised the chiefs by releasing the Indians that he had captured at Bushy Run who were locked up in the jail at the fort. It was a most welcomed gesture of peace. The Indians were pleased.

Colonel Bouquet gathered his officers together after releasing the prisoners and told them,

"All those who volunteered to assist us on this campaign are to be commended and released so that they might return to their homes as quickly as possible. If they know any of the prisoners, they are free to take them home. We will provide everyone with enough food for their journeys.

"I am going to leave a small force here to enforce the peace and take the rest back with me to Ligonier, Bedford and Carlisle. We will take all the former prisoners who have not been identified and find a way to return them to their homes from these locations.

"The horses the Indians provided to send the captives here can be used to help transport the women and children. If there are enough, the sickly men will ride and then the weak. The men who were released and are able to walk will have to march along with the army.

"We will rest here for one week and leave by the same route we took to get here. Make preparations for the horses, food and provisions for the men. Oh, and save two good mounts and saddles for me."

The men rose, left the room and began to delegate responsibilities to their subordinates.

The word of the planned departure spread throughout the fort very quickly. Everyone was excited. The officers were given the task of deciding who would return back east and who would stay at the fort. Some of those who had been there during the siege asked if they could rotate out. Others were happy to stay now that there was peace.

CHAPTER THIRTY-THREE

On the 26th of November, Colonel Bouquet prepared his army for departure. He asked for the two horses he had requested. They were brought to him. He walked to the middle of the parade ground and called for Gus to report to him. Gus broke ranks with the scouts and ran to the Colonel. As the Colonel mounted one of the horses, he handed the reins from the other one to Gus and said "Gus, because you are a scout I cannot promote you, but I can give you this horse as a gift for your outstanding service. Thank you."

Then he saluted and Gus returned the salute. He climbed into the saddle and the two men led the army out of the fort. They were followed by the scouts and then by the Highlanders playing their pipes and drums. The militias came next along with the volunteers who were making their way east, the former prisoners and finally the rest of the 60th Regiment of Foot. Those who were left at Fort Pitt waved goodbye and the army responded with waves as well. They all knew that history had been made. The tide had been turned. Peace had come and the residents of Pittsboro no longer lived in fear.

Within a few days, the army made its way back to the Bushy Run outpost and stopped there to rest and drink deeply from the cool waters. Most of the wounded soldiers who had been left behind had healed well enough to rejoin the ranks and march back east. As the army continued, they passed the battlefield where they had lost comrades nearly four months earlier. As they passed, they noticed markers on the graves of their fallen comrades. The Barleys and other local settlers had made the sight a cemetery for those who had died in the battle and those who had died later as a result of their wounds. All of the men were deeply moved as they passed by. Colonel Bouquet ordered the column to face left and salute; this simple gesture served both as a sign of honor to those who had died and an opportunity to be grateful that those walking by had not suffered their same fate. Some of the former prisoners were touched by the number of people whose lives were given to save them. They once again began to weep, seeing the visible evidence of the sacrifice that had been made.

That night, as the army made camp, Sergeant Caldwell was once again telling stories. This time the story was of the battle of Bushy Run. His audience was the rescued prisoners. He recounted how they had come over the mountain with the heavy wagons of flour and how Colonel Bouquet had sent all the horses to Fort Ligonier ahead of time to carry the bags of flour instead of using the cumbersome wagons. Then he told them how they had been watched and how the scouts had caught the Indians who were spying on them. Finally, he told them about the ambush and how the men had fought so bravely. He even told them about how Gus shot the Indian and took care of him, and how eventually that Indian was instrumental in establishing the peace. Some of the other soldiers added their comments to the commentary and the battle was presented from several vantage points.

One of the young women who had been rescued by Captain Lewis and his men from Virginia told them how she had been taken from her family. She told them a particularly gruesome account of how the Indians had killed her father and brother and scalped them. She said, "While we stopped to rest the first night of my captivity, after the Indians had finished their supper, they got out some scalps, and began to prepare to work with them. They strung them over small hoops which they prepared for that purpose, and then began to dry and scrape them by the fire. They held them to the fire till they were partly dried, and then, with their knives, commenced scraping off the flesh; in that way they continued to work, alternately drying and scraping them, until they were dry and clean. When they finished that part of the task, the Indians combed the hair, painted it and the edges of the scalps, red. Those scalps were from my family. I saw them every day hanging from the pole outside the lodge of the Indians who killed my father and brother. After several years, I never thought I would see my old home again. You cannot imagine how I feel to be free."

Gus heard what she had said. He remembered his own parents with their scalps taken lying on the floor of the cabin. But he realized that he was no longer enraged. He was sad; sad to have lost his parents; sad to think that they would never see him get married or see their grandchildren, but he no longer burned inside for revenge. Perhaps the battles had taken care of that need. Perhaps having killed others himself, he realized that taking another life to get even is not the answer. He wondered. He remembered the words of Mr. Good as they fished by the river in Bedford and envisioned a country full of blind toothless people! This made him smile, showing all his teeth.

CHAPTER THIRTY-FOUR

The next day, the army reached Fort Ligonier. The leaves on the trees around the fort had turned their autumn colors of red, yellow and orange. Some had already fallen and the soldiers made more noise than usual as they rustled through them. The scene was far different than it had been four months earlier. The beauty of this place with the mountain as a backdrop impressed Gus. He thought for a few moments about what it would be like to live here. There was the river for fishing and the woods for hunting and plenty of land for farming. Then he wondered what Elizabeth might think about it. He knew what her father thought. But what would she think? He wondered.

The news of the army coming to Fort Ligonier had spread. Local families from Maryland and Pennsylvania who had loved ones taken over the past years came to the fort to see if they could recognize any of the former prisoners. By the time the army arrived, there were nearly a hundred extra people waiting in the parade ground to watch the army come in.

Colonel Burd was waiting for Colonel Bouquet and as he entered the fort, gave him a smart salute and a warm smile.

"Congratulations, Sir. The reports I have heard indicate that you have been successful beyond all expectations!"

"I would not go that far, but we were able to relieve the fort and bring about peace," replied Colonel Bouquet. "You played a part in the success by serving as a staging place before the battle. You are to be commended for your good work. I have to say that the militias and the men from Pennsylvania who made up the 60th impressed me with their bravery. I knew what the Highlanders were made of, but I was not so sure about the local men."

"I see that the rumors were true about you demanding the captives for peace," said Colonel Burd as the former captives rode and walked into the fort.

"Yes, but in some of the cases, the children who were taken when they were young do not remember their last name or where they lived. It is terribly sad. I plan to stop in Bedford as well and spread the word that the prisoners are free. Perhaps someone will recognize these poor lost children. Please have all the former captives form a line once they get into the fort and then ask the people who have come from the area to pass by and ask any questions they may have in an effort to identify the poor captives."

"Yes sir. I will see to it."

Colonel Burd gave the appropriate instructions and former captives lined up while the local settlers came by one at a time and asked their names, where they had lived, the names of family members or relatives that might help them identify the people they sought. Some of the settlers asked if the former captives had seen or known a particular person they were looking for.

The scenes from the reunions at Fort Pitt were duplicated here at Fort Ligonier. A neighbor recognized a teen age girl whose parents had been killed when she was a child. Several of the men knew each other. But most of the little children did not remember enough of their former lives to help anyone identify them. Many of the older children could remember and were helpful with the little ones if they had been taken at the same time or were living in the same village after they were taken.

There was much happiness for those who had been reunited and for those who had not been identified, there was a feeling of dread that perhaps they had been brought back to a place where no one knew or cared about them. While most of the young ones were captives, they held out hope that one day they would see their families again. Some of them had seen their parents killed and for them, they hoped that a neighbor or relative might find them and give them a new home.

After the two sides had asked and answered questions and established the identities of some of the former prisoners, the visitors began to make their way home and the former captives began to find a place to relax along with the soldiers.

Gus had been watching the local settlers ask their questions and had seen the responses from the former prisoners. When it was over, he felt sad for those who had been left behind. He knew how they felt to be left.

Colonel Burd saw Gus standing there in the parade ground with his horse and asked, "Who was that riding in with you sir? The young man dressed like an Indian."

"Oh, his name is Gus. He signed on as a scout back in Bedford. He has been of great value to me throughout this campaign. He is very good with a musket and saved Captain Barrett's life, and probably that of others, when the scouting party was trying to determine where the Indians villages were located west of Fort Pitt. He also wounded a Delaware chief's son and kept him alive, so we traded him for peace. Yes, Gus started this campaign a young man with no experience as a scout, but I would trust him to help me lead an army anywhere."

"Yes," said Colonel Burd. "When the men you sent back to tell us about the battle came by, I believe they mentioned his name. They said he had been wounded but had also killed an Indian or two in the battle."

"Yes. He came to get me when the scouts were ambushed. Then he wounded the one Indian and killed another two. He also hunted for game and won a contest by not only bringing back the biggest buck, but by saving the other scout's life during a mountain lion attack. He learned the Indian's language and overheard valuable information that I used to persuade the chief's son to lead us to his village. And finally, he killed three more Indians when he saved Captain Barrett."

"Why is he wearing those Indian clothes?" asked Colonel Burd.

"Well," replied Colonel Bouquet, "they were given to him by the mother of the boy he had shot as a way of thanking him for returning her son."

"Well, I can certainly see why you think so highly of the young man, but why does he ride a horse?"

"Since I cannot promote a scout and I already gave him a pay raise, I thought that he might be able to use a good horse when he gets home. I am hoping to convince him to sign up for the 60th Regiment of Foot. He would be a good soldier."

As Colonel Bouquet and Colonel Burd walked inside to the Colonel's office, the rest of the army began to unpack and find a place to rest. Most of the men leaned against the inner walls of the fort, under the walkway that enabled men to fire out over the top of the walls if attacked. Gus had to take care of his horse. He noticed when he dismounted that his feet were not sore like they had been when he marched over the mountains four months earlier, but now, his behind was sore from all those miles in a saddle. He decided that perhaps when they left for the next leg of the return trip, he could walk his horse some and ride it some. That would be good for both man and horse.

He led the horse to the stables. It was a gelding and stood about 15 hands high. It was light brown with a white star and white stockings. Gus had not given him a name yet, but was thinking about one as he began to remove the saddle and brush the horse down. He got some oats to feed it and a bucket of water for it to drink. When he finished brushing, and the horse finished eating, Gus reached into his haversack, pulled out an apple he had been saving and gave it to the horse. White foam oozed out of its mouth as he chomped away at the apple. Gus laughed at how quickly the little treat was consumed. Then he turned the horse loose in the corral and went off to relax and get something to eat.

The cooking fires were soon aglow and the men and women were all busy preparing meals. The little fort was crowded with all the people and Gus was tempted to find a place outside to sleep, but the temperature was colder here and he thought it might frost. He decided to find the other scouts and bed down beside them next to a fire to help keep him warm. When he found Captain Barrett, they began talking about their future plans. The Captain said, "My men and I will rest here a day or two and then head southeast back into Maryland and Fort Cumberland. It should not take us too long to get from here to Cumberland."

"Well sir," said Gus, "it has sure been a pleasure to meet you and to march by your side. You saved my life back at Bushy Run. For that I will always be grateful."

"You returned the favor when that hunting party snuck back around and tried to ambush us. Thanks to you, we still have hair to comb," replied Captain Barrett.

The men laughed and shook hands. They had endured the hardships of war and had both been wounded and faced death, only to be saved by each other. As a result, there was closeness between them not shared by many people.

Gus rolled out his blanket and covered himself up. As he lay on his back looking up at the stars, he continued to recall all that had happened from the time he left Fort Bedford. It had been an amazing time. Now he was only a few days away from returning to Bedford, his aunt and uncle, neighbors and friends. He imagined how it would be going home again. His thoughts turned to Elizabeth. What would he do? What would he say? He knew that he wanted to hold her, tell her that he loved her and never wanted to be away from her again. But, what about the good Reverend? He had not figured out what to do about his request to leave Elizabeth alone. He covered his face with his hat and slowly fell asleep as he tried to come up with an answer.

CHAPTER THIRTY-FIVE

The next day the army rested while the Colonel once again got a report from Colonel Burd on the supplies and the conditions at the Fort. Gus took the opportunity to look around outside the fort. He asked Rodger Johnson, one of the other scouts from Bedford, to go with him as he walked the parameter and made his way down to the river. The water was cool. Leaves were floating by having dropped off the branches of the trees that lined the banks of the river. The mountains to the east were large and beautiful with their fall colors. They wandered to the riverbank and tried to look into the water to see the fish. Finally, Gus decided to try to catch a few for lunch. He cut a branch from a tree and ran back to the fort to get the string and hook he had packed in his haversack just for this purpose. Then the men looked for worms under rocks and rotten limbs. They took turns fishing and before too long were able to catch some brook trout that they cleaned and cooked over a fire Gus built along the bank. Rodger was a big man with a big appetite. He ate three fish by himself. Gus could only eat two. But they continued to fish until they ran out of bait and took the rest of the fish back to the fort to share with the others.

The men relaxed the rest of the day and occupied themselves with chores around the fort. At supper time, the scouts began to realize that the next morning half of their group would be leaving and heading to Cumberland. There was a sense of loss that they were all feeling. They had been through a lot together. Soon one of them started retelling the story of finding the Indians that had been spying on them.

"That Indian just let out a cry and was set on taking as many of us with him as he could. They must believe that the Great Spirit gives some special reward for folks who die in battle or something."

Another scout accused the rest of not paying attention and walking right into the ambush at Bushy Run. Then they remembered the scout that had been killed there.

"We have had some time of it haven't we fellas?" asked one of the men.

"We have that," replied another.

The scouts agreed that they had shared in an experience they would never forget. But now, those from Bedford were heading home and in a few days, the army would need them no more and they could return to their normal activities. The men all seemed to get quiet as they thought about what lie before them. For some it was a return to their families. For others, it was a return to the solitude of a trapper. Gus was once again confronted with what he had to return to. He could not imagine going back to cleaning rooms and tables at the inn. No, now was the time to begin anew. The question was what would he do and how would he do it? Would Elizabeth be his wife or would he be on his own? He had about a week to decide before the army would march into Fort Bedford. Gus told himself that a week would be enough time.

The next morning, the army got an early start and moved out heading east to the mountains. Gus rode for the first two hours and after they stopped for a rest, decided to walk for the next two. As he walked along beside his horse, he tried to think of an appropriate name for him. He considered "Star" because of the white star on his head. Then he thought about "Socks" because of the white stocking on his legs. Finally he gave up and decided to call him "Horse".

The army soon passed the sharp bend where the scouts had found the Indian spies, but without wagons carrying bags of flour, the going was much easier for both man and beast. The climb up the western slope was not so bad and the views were spectacular now that Gus had time to look over the valleys instead of looking for signs of Indians laying in wait.

They reached the top of Blue Mountain and decided to stop there for the night. The western sky was red as the sun was beginning to set. It promised to be a nice day again tomorrow. The army and former captives started to gather wood and prepare their fires. The mood was light this evening and a couple of the men began to play some harmonicas. Soon, people gathered around and singing erupted. Toes began to tap and feet began to stomp. Before the evening was over, some of the men were asking some of the women to dance. It was a little awkward at first, but everyone realized that the dancing was all in good fun. There was a big yellow moon in the sky that helped light up the area so that it was easy to see. Gus asked the little ten-year-old he had danced with at Fort Pitt to be his partner once again. They moved in and out of the squares and swung on each other's arms along with the older people who were doing the same. After a dance or two, Gus asked the three Lowery sisters to dance, but they did not know how and they told him to ask Mrs. McCord who was with them when they were rescued at Bushy Run. Gus did ask her and he had a grand time dancing the square dances and doing whatever the caller told them to do. He was not the best dancer and he stepped on the poor lady's feet on numerous occasions. But they laughed about it and continued to dance.

After a few hours, the musicians were tired and the dancers were exhausted. They all knew they would sleep well that night. The air was crisp at this altitude. The moon and the stars shining down lent an air of peace and tranquility to the late night festivities. The camp settled down into soft conversations and good night wishes as people went about finding a place to sleep.

Gus decided to check on Horse to see how he was doing. He came to the tether line where he had tied him earlier and gave him a rub on his nose and ears. Then he produced another apple and the big horse chomped down his late night snack.

Gus made his way back to the area where the scouts were bedded down and was soon curled up in his blanket asleep.

CHAPTER THIRTY-SIX

After a few more days of marching, Gus began to recognize the area as that where he had lived. The road the army was marching on was near the Juniata River that ran eventually right next to Fort Bedford. The closer he got, the more anxious Gus became. He had not decided what he was going to do about Elizabeth. Perhaps he would see how she and her family reacted to his return. That may give him a clue about what he should do. If they were welcoming, then he would talk to Rev. McGregor about seeing his daughter. On the other hand, if they were not, perhaps he would just get his money and buy some land. Perhaps he would go back over the mountain to Ligonier and clear some land and start his life anew. Yes, those would be the choices. He could not imagine seeing Elizabeth and not being able to share his life with her.

About a mile away from the fort, Colonel Bouquet instructed the Highlanders to strike up a march on the pipes and drums. The other musicians in the militias played along. The army looked sharp as it made its way toward the fort. The sentries announced the arrival and the main gate was flung open wide for the returning heroes.

Gus had fallen back a little to ride Horse in with the other scouts from Bedford. Colonel Bouquet led the army into the fort. As he entered the gates, cheers rang out in such volume that Gus and all of the others knew there were more people gathered behind the walls of the fort than the men who were left behind to protect it four months earlier. The men straightened up as they heard the cheers. They assumed the welcome had come from the people who lived in the little town and the surrounding area. Most of the scouts had family who would be cheering and waiting for them to enter the fort.

Gus and Horse entered the fort and he was not sure if he should look around for people he knew or not. He decided to look straight ahead and not act like he was anxious to see anyone in particular. As he passed by some of the crowd, he heard his name called. He turned to see the person who had called to him and there stood his aunt and uncle. He waved and continued to move ahead with the army that was filling up the inside of the fort. Again he heard his name called and this time he recognized the voice. It was George. Gus gave him a big smile and waved to him as he continued on into the parade ground. Finally, Gus and the scouts could go no farther. He dismounted and stood there holding Horse by the reins. The cheers of the crowd were all around him. The people seemed ever so grateful for the job the army had done and the resulting end of hostilities. As he stood soaking in the cheers and waves and words of congratulations, he saw someone moving through the crowd in his direction. In an instant he felt himself grow flush. He knew before he could confirm it that the person coming his way was Elizabeth. She was pushing her way through the crowd and finally when she broke free, ran the last five steps and threw her arms around Gus' neck.

"I'm happy to say I'll be able to speak to you again." she said and then she kissed him right on the lips. The kiss was even better than anything Gus had ever imagined. He held her tight and lifted her off the ground and swung her around in joy. Finally he stopped and put her down, but he did not stop hugging her. They continued their embrace as they both tried to talk at once.

Gus said, "I missed you every day."

Elizabeth said, "Are you alright? Your letter said you were hurt!"

They laughed and hugged some more. This time Gus gave the kiss and Elizabeth pressed herself fully into his embrace and sighed.

After a moment George and Gus' aunt and uncle were also by his side. His uncle cleared his throat to get the attention of the two young people who were obviously very happy to see each other. Gus and Elizabeth reluctantly broke free from each other long enough for Gus to hug his aunt shake hands with his uncle and accept pats on his back from George.

"Where did you get the horse?" asked George.

"Colonel Bouquet gave it to me" replied Gus. The others looked at him in amazement.

"Why would he do that?" asked his uncle.

"Oh, it was just his way of saying thanks, I guess."

"He is a beauty," said George. "What's his name?"

"I just call him Horse."

Everyone laughed at that.

George said, "That's not very original."

Even Gus had to agree, it was not a very good name.

"Well, you all come up with a better one and I'll use it."

"How about Destiny?" asked a new voice.

Gus turned to look at the person who made the suggestion. It was Rev. McGregor.

"Welcome home Gus." he said with his hand extended. "I believe from what I've heard about your exploits during this campaign that you are destined to become a great man."

"Thank you sir, but I'm not interested in greatness."

"Yes, but greatness is interested in you."

Mrs. McGregor interrupted the conversation by pushing in and giving Gus a hug and a peck on the cheek.

"I do believe you have lost some weight while you've been away. You need to come by often for some good home cooking young man!" Then she gave him a wink and stepped back into the circle surrounding Gus and his horse.

The group all seemed to have questions for Gus and he tried to answer them as quickly as they came.

Elizabeth was first. "What about the wound we heard about? Are you alright?"

"Yes. During the first day of the Battle at Bushy Run, a musket ball grazed my arm. It has already healed. It did not stop me from doing my part."

"From what we hear, you did more than your part", said his uncle.

George asked, "Why did you save that Indian's life?"

"You mean Newate? I can't say why, but after I shot him, I felt like I needed to help him. In the end, he helped us bring about peace with his father's tribe of Delaware Indians. His parents thought he was dead, and when we brought him back, they were very grateful. In fact, his mother gave me this buckskin outfit here in my haversack." Gus got it out and showed it to them, they all agreed it was a very nice gift.

"I understand you saved a few lives out there Gus" said Rev. McGregor.

"Yes sir, I guess I did, but that's what you do in an army. I had mine saved once too by Captain Barrett who was the leader of the scouts."

"What happened?" cried Elizabeth.

"Well, this big Indian came at me with his tomahawk. He was screaming and painted up with red and black paint. I was scared and fired, but only wounded him. I'm sure he would have killed me had not Captain Barrett fired over my shoulder and put a ball into his head."

At that point, Colonel Bouquet and Lieutenant Carre came walking by. Colonel Bouquet nodded to Gus and asked, "Is this your family?"

Gus introduced everyone.

"It's my pleasure to meet all of you. Gus here has been a fine scout for us."

"Yes, he was just telling us how Captain Barrett saved his life in the battle." said George.

"Did he tell you about catching Indian spies as we were making our way to Fort Ligonier?"

"No."

"Did he tell you how he ran back under heavy fire from the ambush to let me know what was happening so I could plan my counter attack?"

"No."

"Did he tell you about the Indian he shot and tied up and cared for?"

"Yes. He told us in a letter, but didn't give us much detail"

"Did he tell you about learning the Indian language and listening in on the conservations of those we held prisoner?"

"Yes, he said in that letter that he was learning some." replied Gus' uncle.

"Can you speak Indian?" asked George

"Yes, I learned a little."

"Did he tell you about the scouting party and how he saved many lives when Indians tried to sneak around them to ambush them in Ohio?"

"No."

"Captain Barrett had been wounded and Gus killed three Indians in that skirmish. He saved the Captain's life. That little deed earned him that horse."

"Did I miss anything, Gus?"

"Yes you did," replied a nearby scout. "Pardon the intrusion, Sir. Did he tell you how he killed the mountain lion and saved my life?"

"No."

"Well he did, and in the process, won a bet by bringing home the biggest buck in all of western Pennsylvania."

"Well Gus, it seems to me that you've got a lot of explaining to do," said Colonel Bouquet.

The group gathered around him looked at him with admiring smiles and expected to hear all about his adventure, but Gus just said, "I think there has been some exaggeration. I didn't do anything any of the rest of the men wouldn't do. We had a mission and we accomplished it. And now, I'm glad it's over."

"It sounds to me like you fulfilled your promise to avenge your parents' deaths. You killed some Indians," said Gus' uncle.

"In the battle and the skirmish, I was not thinking about revenge. I was trying to stay alive. I was scared to death. After I got to know the Indians better, I found out that they are not all bad. They want to live in peace as much as we do."

"Well, Gus," said Rev. McGregor, "when we heard the reports of the battle and now that we hear even more about your behavior, it seems like I may have been too hasty to make a judgment resulting in our last conversation. Anyone who would risk his life for peace and save the lives of others is a man of great character. That is far more important than occupation. And besides, there is one young lady in my household who has been praying for your safe return daily. You are welcome to come by to visit any time."

Rev. McGregor reached out his hand one more time and shook hands with Gus. Elizabeth started to cry and gave Gus another hug.

CHAPTER THIRTY-SEVEN

The drums rolled and the noise of the homecoming soon died down. Colonel Bouquet stepped forward and said, "I do not wish to take too much time away from this celebration, but knowing that our scouts will not be continuing on with us to Carlisle, I wanted to take this opportunity to thank them for the good work they did. They captured two Indians who were spying on us and scouted out the various Indian villages in the Ohio Territory so that we knew where to go and the strength of their tribes. For their good work, I am grateful. The community of Bedford should be proud of your men. I would like to offer them all an opportunity to serve with the Royal Americans."

The crowd cheered for the men, the offer and the army.

Colonel Bouquet continued, "One particular young man is to be commended for his bravery, resourcefulness, marksmanship and his sense of human decency. He saved the lives of many of our men, and the life of any enemy. In so doing, he helped bring about a peace that may have saved many lives on both sides. I would like to present to him this Medal of Honor. Gustave Giron, please step forward."

The crowd applauded, whistled and shouted as Gus slowly made his way to the front. As he walked he got the overwhelming sensation that his parents were walking slowly beside him. Each had their arm around his waist as if to support him. Tears filled his eyes and yet he smiled realizing that their memory would continue to support him in whatever direction his life would take.

Colonel Bouquet gave Gus the medal and shook his hand. Gus turned to face the crowd and held the medal up high. He said, "This medal is for all of us who fought. I accept it on behalf of myself and everyone else, especially those who lost their lives for peace."

Once again the crowd applauded. Gus returned to Elizabeth's side and she squeezed his hand with pride and tears in her eyes.

"I would also like to take some time to ask each of the women and children who were taken prisoner to form a line over on the right side wall, and invite you towns-people to go by them and ask questions to try to see if you know them or know anything that can help us find their families. Some of these poor souls were taken as children and do not remember their parents," said Colonel Bouquet.

Towns-people and family members came to see if they recognized any of them as their mothers, wives, daughters or sisters. One particular mother stood back and looked at the girls. It had been two years since she had been taken. But she did not recognize anyone as her daughter.

"I don't see my Regina." she told the Colonel.

"Are you sure?" replied Colonel Bouquet. "Do you remember if she had any particular birth marks or anything that would help us identify her?"

"No", Mrs. Leininger replied, "none that I can remember."

The Colonel seemed to be out of suggestions. He was about to move to the next person to see if they could find their loved one when Gus said,

"Excuse me Sir, perhaps the girl had a favorite song or bed-time story that might make a connection."

The mother's face lit up and she began to sign an old German hymn she had sung to her little daughter years ago.

"Allein und doch nicht gnaz alleine.

Bin ich in meiner Einsamkeit."

Just then a tall, thin girl, dressed like an Indian with braided hair, stepped out of the line and began to sing along.

"Denn Wenn ich ganz verlassen scheine,
Vertrebt mir Jesus selbst die Zeit,

Ich bin bei ihm und er bei mir,
So kommt mir's gar nicht einsam fur."

Mother and daughter were reunited. With tears of joy they clung to each other and swayed back and forth. With Regina was a small child that she had been forced to carry when the Indians took them years earlier. No one came for this child and so, Mrs. Leininger agreed to take them both with her to Tulpechocken where she lived.

"Good God," said George, "Its Regina Leininger. Do you remember I told you that story Gus?"

"Yes. That reunion made the marching and fighting worthwhile."

The young men stood and watched in amazement as mother and daughter clung to each other.

Gus turned to Elizabeth and said, "One day I would like a daughter, and maybe a son too."

"Don't you need a wife first?"

"Yes, I'm going to have to work on that. What do you think about a farmer for a husband?"

"So long as that farmer is you, I think that would be just fine."